Month-by-Month Phonics for Second Grade
Second Edition

by
Dorothy P. Hall
and Patricia M. Cunningham

Carson-Dellosa Publishing Company, Inc.
Greensboro, North Carolina

This book is dedicated to second-grade teachers everywhere and especially to those teachers who shared ideas with us and whose superb teaching inspired the writing of this book. We learned from the questions you posed and the solutions you offered.

–Dottie and Pat

Credits

Editors
Bernadette Batliner
Joey Bland

Layout Design
Van Harris

Inside Illustrations
Lori Jackson
Nick Greenwood

Cover Design
Van Harris

Cover Photos
© 1997 Comstock, Inc.
© 2002 Brand X Pictures

Table of Contents

Introduction

How do you feel about the phonics part of your second-grade curriculum? Do you look forward to teaching phonics each day? More importantly, how do your students feel about phonics? Do they look forward to their daily dose of phonics instruction?

If thinking about these questions makes you visualize stacks of worksheets, flash cards, and phonics drills, you need this book.

In all teaching, but particularly in teaching phonics, the "how" is as important as the "what." The "what" of phonics instruction is clear and not open to debate. Second graders need fast, fluent, and automatic recognition of the most frequently used words. Simultaneously, they need to develop strategies that allow them to quickly decode less-common words. When they are reading and writing, they need to apply phonics strategies to read and spell a lot of words. The rapid identification of sight words, the strategies for decoding words, and the application of these strategies when reading and writing are the "what" of phonics instruction.

The "how" of phonics instruction goes back to the questions of how you and your students feel about the phonics activities you do each day. Are they fun for you and your students? Do the activities engage students in physical and mental manipulation of letters and sounds? Can all of your students, including students with special needs and English language learners, participate in and achieve some level of success and satisfaction from the phonics activities? Are the phonics lessons taught in a way that maximizes transfer and application to reading and writing?

Month-by-Month Phonics for Second Grade teaches the same "what" as other second-grade phonics programs, but in a very different way. All of the activities in *Month-by-Month Phonics for Second Grade* were designed to be consistent with the research about motivation, engagement, and transfer. Learners are motivated and engaged when they perceive an activity as fun or enjoyable and when they are able to successfully participate. Learners are motivated and engaged when they can actively participate, physically and mentally, in the activity. Transfer occurs when the activity in which the strategies are taught is closely connected to the activity in which learners need to actually use the strategies. Here are some examples of how the "what" of second-grade phonics is taught in a fun, active, and success- and transfer-oriented way.

Learning to read and spell sight words automatically and fluently is an essential second-grade goal. The major activity for achieving this goal in *Month-by-Month Phonics for Second Grade* is the Word Wall. High-frequency words are gradually added to the wall, and many words that were introduced in first grade are taught again in second grade to make sure that all students can read and spell them. Each day, students are actively engaged in learning these critical words as the teacher leads students to cheer and write the words. Unlike flash cards, which require students to use a visual strategy for learning, the daily Word Wall practice engages the auditory, rhythmic function of the brain as students cheer and the kinesthetic brain function as students write the words. Both the cheering and the writing of these words engage students in active physical participation with the words. All students can succeed in cheering and writing the words because the teacher leads the cheers and models the writing. Transfer is ensured because once words are on the Word Wall and are being practiced daily, students are reminded and required to spell those words correctly in their writing.

Unlike the Word Wall, the goal of the Making Words activity is not to teach sight words. Making Words is a guided activity in which students discover the patterns used for decoding and spelling words. English is not a "one-letter, one-sound" language. The spelling system in English is determined not by individual letters but by patterns of letters. For example, the vowel **a** can represent 16 different sounds, but the patterns—**ay, aw**, **at**, **ate**, **ar**, **ain**, **alk**, **oat**, **eat**—are consistent. In Making Words, students are guided to manipulate letters in such a way that they discover the patterns.

All students can succeed in Making Words because everyone is encouraged to change letters to match the correct word once that word is made in a pocket chart. Success-guaranteed opportunities are included in every lesson since many words require just a small change that all second graders can accomplish. In this example lesson, students have the letters **i**, **p**, **r**, **s**, and **t** and manipulate their letters to make these changes:

"Change the last letter to turn **sit** into **sip**."

"Change the first letter to change **sip** into **rip**."

"Add 1 letter to the front to turn **rip** into **trip**."

Making Words lessons require students' active physical and mental participation. Physically, students manipulate the letters, and mentally, they solve the puzzle of how words are spelled by making small changes. Once the words are made, students physically move the words to sort them into patterns. The transfer step of the Making Words lesson also requires students' physical participation as they write new words based on the patterns sorted for.

Other activities in *Month-by-Month Phonics for Second Grade* also engage students in success- and transfer-oriented participation. Students use beginning-letter sounds, context, and word length to predict the covered words during Guess the Covered Word lessons. They round up the rhymes from favorite books and use these rhymes to spell new words in Rounding Up the Rhymes. In Using Words You Know, they learn how to use simple words and patterns in those words to read and spell other words. Reading/Writing Rhymes offers second graders another way to look at patterns and all of the words they can read and write using simple or complex patterns.

Phonics is an essential part of a balanced reading and writing program in second grade. You can teach phonics in ways that are not boring, repetitive, or far removed from reading and writing. Combining the motivating, successful, and transfer-focused activities in this book with a lot of reading and writing will help you help second graders read and write fluently, eagerly, and well. The activities might even change your answers to the questions that began this introduction. Have fun with your students daily as you use this book to teach phonics each month of the school year!

August/September

Month at a Glance

It's the first day of second grade! Last year's little first graders are now "big" second graders. Students who were successful at learning how to read and write in first grade are anxious to get back to school and learn more! They have had a taste of success, and they like it. They almost demand that their second-grade teacher continue this exciting literacy journey. Other students are just beginning to understand how reading works. If they have been fortunate, they have had kindergarten and first-grade teachers who shared a love of books and stories, and these students are still excited about learning how to read. **Regardless, it is not too late to help second graders and to watch both their size and knowledge grow.**

It is not where these students are on their literacy journeys that matters but that each student makes progress every year! There is no telling how much seven-year-olds can learn in a year when they feel good about themselves and are receiving good instruction that makes sense to them. We have watched many students whom we were worried about in first grade develop into good, solid students in second grade. We have learned that it is never too late for students to learn how to read and write if they think that they can! Your second graders have had some instruction in learning how to read and write, but watch out—summer is over, and they are ready for more!

By the end of the first 4–6 weeks, you will have **reviewed** the following:

- Concepts of print
- Phonemic awareness
- Using students' names to make letter, sound, and word observations
- Beginning-letter sounds
- Rhyming words
- Segmenting words into sounds
- Key names for consonants
- Vowel sounds

You will have **introduced** the following:

- Alphabet books and picture dictionaries to explore beginning sounds for beginning letters
- A Word Wall on which many high-frequency words are displayed
- Rounding Up the Rhymes as a way to focus on spelling patterns
- Guess the Covered Word as a way to cross-check using context, word length, and phonics clues
- Making Words—a three-step, multilevel, manipulative activity

In this chapter, we will describe some **activities for the first 4–6 weeks of second grade that will help you see where students are in their word knowledge—what they know about words and how words work.** These activities will also help students develop critical concepts that they need when reading (decoding) and writing (encoding) and simultaneously convince all students that they are becoming readers and writers. Now, we know that our use of the word **all** has you shaking your head and wondering if we have seen the second-grade classes in your school! While we haven't seen all second-grade classes, we have seen enough to know about what you are worrying. **In most classrooms, there are some students who come to second grade reading quite well, other students who can read but have much more to learn, and still other students who are at the emergent stage.** What can you do during the first 4–6 weeks of school that will meet the needs of this wide range of entering literacy levels found in almost every second-grade class? How can you review with the class and assess students' word knowledge while teaching those who haven't learned important print concepts yet? We will try to answer these questions in this chapter. **Students come to us at different literacy levels, and they must sense that they are making progress if their eagerness and excitement are to sustain them through the hard work of learning how to read.**

Informal Assessment

In second grade, teachers begin the year by informally assessing students as they read and write. Teachers often want to know what the new second graders know and what they will need to be taught this year. Because there is such a wide variety in what students know and can do at this time of year, teachers often begin by looking at the concepts that students need to understand in order to be successful in early reading and writing. For students who already know everything on this list, the assessment is a quick, simple task. For the few students who don't, it is important to know what needs to be taught again in second grade so that all students will find success! Following are some important concepts to look for early in second grade.

Print Concepts

Print is what we read and write. Print includes all of the funny little marks—letters, punctuation, and spaces between words and paragraphs—that translate into familiar spoken language. We read across the page in a left-to-right fashion. When we finish a line, we make a return sweep and start all over again. If there are sentences at the top of a page, a picture in the middle, and more sentences at the bottom, we read the top first and then the bottom. We start at the front of a book and go toward the back.

In addition to learning how to move our eyes to follow print, young students **must also learn the jargon of print. Jargon** refers to all of the words we use to talk about reading and writing and includes terms such as **word**, **letter**, **sentence**, and **sound**. We use this jargon constantly as we try to teach students how to read:

"Look at the **first word** in the **sentence**. How does that **word** begin? What **letter** makes that **sound**?"

Using some jargon is essential to talking with students about reading and writing, but students who don't come from rich literacy backgrounds are often hopelessly confused by this jargon in the early grades. Most second-grade students have a grasp of this jargon, but some students have missed previously taught instruction because they did not understand the jargon and could not take advantage of the instruction at that time.

Although most second graders understand these concepts, it is helpful to have a checklist for students who do not. Many teachers use a checklist like the one shown at right.

Teachers use the checklist as students are reading in a shared-reading format with big books, with a small group during reading, or during a mini-lesson in which they model writing and ask students to help them (shared writing). The teacher asks students who still do not have a grasp of these concepts to point to what they are reading or to show her where she should write. She also asks them if they can point to just one word, to the first and last word, to just one letter, and to the first and last letters of a word. If they are successful, she puts checks in the rows showing what they have demonstrated. **When a student has several checks in a box, the teacher can assume that this student has an understanding of the concept, and she doesn't need to look for this concept anymore. When a student demonstrates that he understands all of these concepts, the teacher draws a line through his name and focuses the instruction and assessment on students who have not yet demonstrated these concepts.** In second grade, this may not take a long time and is well worth the effort for those students who have not yet mastered these concepts. Knowing which students need a little extra nudge allows the teacher to give this help to those who need it when reading and writing.

Concepts of Print Checklist	Tom	Sue	Bob
• Starts on left	✔	✔	✔
• Goes left to right	✔		✔
• Makes return sweep to next line	✔		✔
• Matches words by pointing to each word as reading	✔	✔	✔
• Can point to just one word	✔	✔	✔
• Can point to the first word and the last word	✔		✔
• Can point to just one letter	✔	✔	✔
• Can point to the first letter and the last letter	✔	✔	✔

Phonemic Awareness

Phonemic awareness is the ability to manipulate sounds. Phonemic awareness develops through a series of stages during which students first become aware that language is made up of individual sounds, that words are made up of syllables, and that syllables are made up of phonemes. Students develop phonemic awareness as a result of exposure to oral and written language. Nursery rhymes, chants, and Dr. Seuss books usually play a large role in this development before children start school. Once in school, young students continue to listen to and read stories and hear rhymes and rhyming words. They use what they have learned about letters and sounds when they read and write. These activities help young students see that words are made of sounds and that sounds can be changed to make different words. Only when students realize that words can be changed and how changing a sound changes a word are they able to profit from instruction in phonics, or letter-sound relationships.

Letter Names and Sounds

Most second graders have learned the letter names and can recognize all 26 letters in both upper- and lowercase forms. For those students you are still not sure about, **assess each student's knowledge of letter names and sounds by giving her a sheet of paper on which the letters are listed in random order and asking her to point to all of the letters she knows. For the letters she doesn't know, ask, "Can you tell me what sound this letter makes?"** Note the response with **S** if she knows the **sound**. If she does not have the correct sound for the letter, ask, "Do you know any words that begin with this letter?" Indicate with **W** for **word** any letters for which the student doesn't give names or sounds but for which she has a **word** association.

Word Learning

Most second-grade students who have had reading and writing experiences have learned some words. **To assess their reading abilities, you may want to listen to each student read a book of his or your choice. A good time to do this is during Self-Selected Reading.** Since one book does not fit all in second grade, have several easy and a few difficult first-grade books available. Some teachers have been trained in running records (Clay, 1993) or in giving Informal Reading Inventories (Johns, 2001) and carry out their assessments in this fashion. Other teachers, whose students had a Word Wall in first grade, have students read words from the first-grade Word Wall list (Cunningham, Hall, and Sigmon, 2008). The expectation is not that every student knows all of the words (although some students will), but that every student has learned some words and is adding to this store of words. **Most second graders' reading is measurable, and they are better at reading the words than they are at spelling them.**

Once you get to know your students, you will see that literacy comes more easily for some than others. Find out what your students know so that you can begin to help those who are behind their peers while furthering the literacy journey of others. **Those second graders who do not have a strong sense of how words work need to focus their attention on letter names and** sounds. **Students who have phonemic awareness can tell you when words begin with the same sound. When they have learned something about phonics, they can tell you what letter makes that sound.** The following Getting to Know You activities offer several ways to get acquainted with your students while you help other students develop or improve their phonemic awareness and letter-sound relationships.

What Is Multilevel Instruction?

You can use many multilevel Getting to Know You activities at the beginning of the year to introduce students to each other and to find out what these new second graders know about words. **A multilevel activity is one in which there are multiple things to be learned and multiple ways for students to move forward.**

Getting to Know You

Getting to Know You is a way to meet all of your students and review letters and sounds (including blends, digraphs, and vowel sounds). Here are some activities you can use with students:

Name Cheers

Select five students to cheer for each day. Let their names be the first words on your Word Wall. (More information about the Word Wall can be found on page 16.) Have each student lead her name's cheer, pointing to each letter in her name and saying it. For example, Sharon would say, "Give me an **S**. Give me an **h**. Give me an **a**," and so on. Finish each name cheer by chanting all of the letters in the name and shouting the student's name. **Students learn letter names quickly when they associate them with the names of their classmates and have cheered them in a rhythmic fashion.** Let them write these five names, one at a time after the chanting and cheering, on a half sheet of writing paper. Students who know the letter names and the names of their classmates are also practicing handwriting. This skill needs to be reviewed at the beginning of the year and practiced daily throughout the year. In this way, you can accomplish two goals at once!

Letter Sorts

Use large index cards or sections of sentence strips with students' names written on them and give them to students. Point to one letter and have each student who has that letter anywhere in his name come to the front of the classroom. Count to see how many names have that letter. Next, have these students divide themselves into first letter, last letter, or somewhere in between. Count again. Have students say each name—stretching out the letters to hear the sounds. Decide if the letter has its usual sound. For example, the letter **s** has its usual sound in **Samantha** and **Jason** but not in **Sharon**.

Reviewing Beginning Sounds

So far, the activities described would be most appropriate in kindergarten or first grade (although many second graders—particularly dual-language students—could benefit greatly from these activities). Second-grade teachers can also use the names of their students to review and teach important word concepts. With younger students, use only first names, but for second-graders, you may want to include last names. **Students need to understand that although letters have predictable sounds, they may have more than one sound.** For this activity, **focus on names that do not begin with vowels. First, sort the names according to the beginning letters—everything up to the first vowel. Then, have students say the names and divide any names whose beginning letters have different sounds.** In the chart below are the names of students whose names begin with **C**. Once the names are sorted, help students see that sometimes, as in **Craig, Crosby, Crystal, Clarissa,** and

Cathy Carlos Connor	Cindy Cybill	Chad Chelsea	Craig Crosby Crystal	Clay Clarissa

Clay, the beginning letters are blended together. Other times, such as in **Chad** and **Chelsea,** letter combinations, such as **ch,** have special sounds. The most common sound of **c** is at the beginning of **Cathy, Carlos,** and **Connor** but **c** can also have the /s/ sound, as in **Cindy** and **Cybill.** Some students might have a simplistic notion that all beginning letters always have the same sounds, and they look at only the first letter and guess the word. **This activity reviews beginning sounds, including the importance of looking at all of the letters up to the first vowel.** Second graders do not consider this activity to be boring and babyish when they are thinking about their names and the names of their friends.

Clapping Syllables

The first way that students learn to pull apart words is by breaking them into syllables. Say each student's name and have students clap the beats in that name as they say it with you. Help them see that **Jay** and **Pat** are one-beat names, **Jessie** and **Ryan** have two beats, **Ebony** and **Stephanie** have three beats, and so on. Once students begin to understand syllables, clap the beats and have each student whose name has that number of beats stand up and say his name as he claps the beats with you.

Matching Beginning Sounds

Say a sound—not a letter name—and have all of the students whose names begin with that sound come forward. Stretch out the sound as you make it. For the /s/ sound, **Samantha, Sarah, Steven,** and **Cedric** should all come forward. Have everyone stretch out the /s/ as they say the names. If anyone points out that **Cedric** starts with **c** or that Steven starts with **st,** explain that they are correct about the letters, but that now they are just listening for sounds.

··

Hearing Rhyming Words

Call on students whose names have a lot of rhyming words, such as **Will**, **Pat**, and **Mike**. Say a word that rhymes with one of the names and have students say the word and the rhyming name.

Segmenting Words into Sounds

Stretch out students' names, emphasizing each letter. Have each student line up when she hears her name. As each student lines up, have the class stretch out the name with you. Can students hear and write the letters they hear at the beginning, in the middle, and at the end of each name?

Key Names for Consonants

Using a roll of bulletin board paper, make a banner with all of the consonant letters, common blends, consonant digraphs (**ch**, **sh**, **th**, and **wh**), **c /s/**, and **g /j/**. Under each letter or letters, write the name of every student in your class whose name starts with that onset. For some beginning letters, you will not have examples. With your students, brainstorm the names of people that begin with that onset/sound and add a few names so that every letter has at least one key name displayed with it.

It is important to include the blends and digraphs on your banner because struggling readers often use only the first letter when trying to decode or spell a word. When students are reading or writing and they do not use the correct beginning sound or use only one of the beginning letters, refer them to the key-name banner.

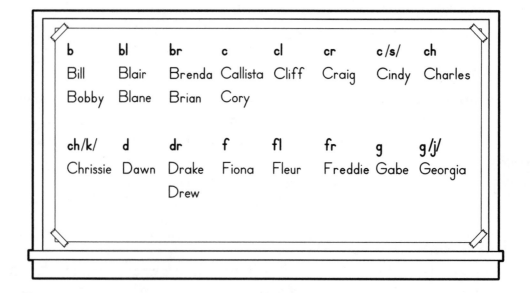

Vowel Posters
(6 sessions—1 vowel per session)

The vowels, of course, are harder, and struggling students are usually confused by all of the jargon and rules that they have not been able to learn. With struggling students, avoid talking about whether a vowel is long, short, or r-controlled. Rather, try to get them to use vowel sounds in words they know to figure out other words. In every class, students' names will provide a lot of examples for the common sounds of each vowel. Using poster board, make a chart for each vowel (including **y** when it's used as a vowel, as in Cathy) on which you list all of your students' names that contain that vowel. Highlight the vowel in each name that matches the vowel heading for that column.

Read the names on each poster with students, emphasizing the sound of the highlighted vowel. Cross through any vowels that are silent. When students are reading and having difficulty decoding a word, direct their attention to the appropriate name, saying something like, "Try the sound of **o** that you hear in **Donna**."

a	e	i	o	u	y
Charles	Charles	Mike	Donna	Octavius	Cathy
Catherine	Catherine	Catherine	Octavius	Justin	Ryan
Donna	Cedric	Cedric	Carol		Danny
Octavius	Mike	Justin			
Danny		Octavius			
Carol					
Ryan					

How Getting to Know You Is Multilevel
During the first weeks of school, you want to get to know your students and review (or teach) some of the previously taught concepts. Using students' names is the perfect way to accomplish both goals. Second graders are interested in themselves and their classmates! You may choose from the Getting to Know You activities. What you choose depends on your class. Some teachers will choose one or two activities and feel good about their classes. Other teachers will have to do more.

30 min.

Alphabet Books and Picture Dictionaries

There are many wonderful alphabet books to read and enjoy. Many of these books fit nicely into your themes or units. Research shows that simple books without many words on a page and with pictures that most students recognize are the most helpful in building students' letter-sound and letter-name knowledge. Once the book has been read and reread several times, students will enjoy reading it during Self-Selected Reading time. **It is very important that students have time to choose and read books each day.** Simple alphabet books that have been read together are books that students can read on their own before they can read books with more text.

Alphabet Books

Here are a few alphabet books that meet our criteria:

A My Name Is Alice by Jane Bayer (Dial, 1984)

All Aboard ABC by Doug Magee and Robert Newman (Dutton Juvenile, 1990)

Animalia by Graeme Base (Harry N. Abrams, 1987)

Annie, Bea, and Chi Chi Dolores: A School Day Alphabet by Donna Maurer (Orchard Books, 1993)

Basketball ABC: The NBA Alphabet by Florence Cassen Mayers (Harry N. Abrams, 1996)

Bugs and Beasties ABC by Cheryl Nathan (Cool Hand Communications, 1995)

Curious George Learns the Alphabet by Margret Rey and H. A. Rey (Houghton Mifflin, 1963)

From Apple to Zipper by Nora Cohen (Aladdin Books, 1993)

From Letter to Letter by Teri Sloat (Dutton Juvenile, 1989)

The Monster Book of ABC Sounds by Alan Snow (Dial, 1991)

NBA Action from A to Z by James Preller (Scholastic, 1997)

The Sweet and Sour Animal Book by Langston Hughes (Oxford University Press, 1994)

Once you and your students have read several alphabet books, you might want to make picture dictionaries with your class. The class works on a few letter pages every day so that by the end of the first month of school, each student has a picture dictionary to use when writing. **Students can recognize the words because they choose the words and draw the pictures.** Brainstorm several words for each letter sound, letting each student decide which words she wants to put at the tops of her pages or sections. All of the **a** words go on one page. Then, **b** words take two pages, with the second page divided in half—for **bl** words and **br** words. The letter **c** takes two pages both divided in half—one page for **c** and **c /s/**; and the other page for **cl** words and **cr** words. Students use the Word Wall for high-frequency words and high-frequency spelling patterns as they write. The picture dictionary is a place for students to write other words that are not high-frequency words but are words that they want to spell correctly and need when writing.

Here are some ideas:

A	alphabet, acorns, animals, adults	**Pl**	plants, plate, plastic, plow
B	books, bags, boys, boxes	**Pr**	principal, prince, pretzels
Bl	blinds, blouses, blocks, blue	**Q**	questions, queen, quilt, quarter
Br	brown, brain, brother, broccoli	**R**	rainbow, red, robin, ride, ring
C	computer, counter, cap, cup	**S**	sink, six, seven, sun, socks
C /s/	city, celery, circus, circle	**Sc**	scale, scab, score, scarf
Ch	children, chowder, chalk, cherries	**Sh**	shoes, shop, shirt, shapes
Cl	class, closet, clothes, clown	**Sk**	skates, sky, skirt, ski
Cr	crowd, crayon, crab, crocodile	**Sl**	slug, sleep, slice, slide
D	desks, door, doctor, dish	**Sm**	smile, smell, smoke, smart
Dr	drawing, drain, dryer, dress	**Sn**	snack, snake, sneakers, snail
E	estimate, egg, eraser, elephant	**Sp**	sponge, spy, spoon, sports
F	feet, fan, father, face	**St**	stories, stone, stem, stick
Fl	flag, fly, flower	**Str**	straw, street, strap, stream
Fr	friend, french fries, frog, frame	**Sw**	sweep, swim, sweets, swing
G	game, girl, goose, gate	**T**	teacher, table, tail, toaster
G /j/	giant, giraffe, gym, general	**Th**	thumb, thimble, thermometer
Gl	glue, glass, glitter, globe	**Thr**	three, throne, thread, throat
Gr	graph, grain, grass, grape	**Tr**	triangle, tricks, train, tray
H	hamster, hat, house, hug	**Tw**	twins, twelve, twenty, twine
I	intercom, igloo, ice, island	**U**	unicorn, umbrella, underwear, unicycle
J	jump, jog, juice, jelly, jam, jar	**V**	violet, vines, vase, vest
K	keys, kangaroo, kite, king	**W**	window, wall, watch, waffle
L	lemon, ladybug, lettuce, light	**Wh**	whistle, white, whopper, whale
M	music, mother, mat, man	**Wr**	wreath, wrist, wrinkle
N	names, nap, night, nickel	**X**	X-ray
O	olive, orange, octopus, ostrich	**Y**	yo-yo, yellow, yawn, yarn
P	pencils, pants, paint, potato	**Z**	zippers, zebras, zero, zoo

···

How Making a Picture Dictionary Is Multilevel

When making individual books with students, you are reviewing letters and the sounds that different letters and letter combinations make. For some students, this activity is important because they do not understand this concept yet. For other students, you are teaching them that certain letters make many sounds depending on the words they are in. The words for each letter and sound are more meaningful for students if they choose which words to write and draw. It is easier for students to remember that a word starts like **muffin** if it is their word of choice rather than a word that someone else has chosen. **A picture dictionary at any grade level is a multilevel activity because different students will write different words depending on their word knowledge and their needs when writing.**

10 min.

Word Wall

A Word Wall is a wall on which words are displayed—but not just any words, only truly important words. Most teachers reserve a bulletin board, wall space, or the space above the board for these important words. Some second-grade teachers begin the Word Wall with students' names because they are important words to second-grade students! (See Name Cheers on page 10.) Regardless of whether you start your Word Wall with the names of your students, the high-frequency words displayed should be the words that second-graders use in reading and writing every day. Provide a brief 5–10 minute review activity of words each day and require students to spell these words correctly when writing. Often, students in second grade have learned to read many high-frequency words but cannot spell the same words correctly when writing. Encoding is a more difficult task than decoding for young students and adults. Recognizing these high-frequency words helps students read; being able to spell high-frequency words helps them write.

Here is a partial sample of what your Word Wall might look like if you add students' names to the Word Wall. The *Word Wall "Plus" for Second Grade* Bulletin Board is available from Carson-Dellosa.

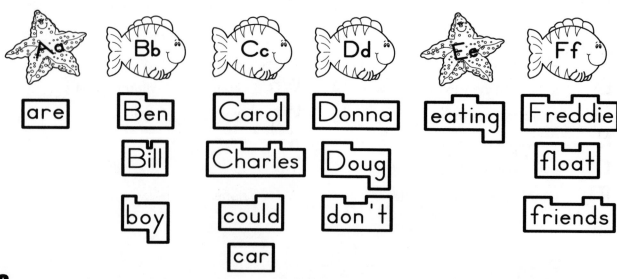

Adding Words to the Word Wall

Add five words to the Word Wall each week. In second grade, base your word selection more on what you observe in students' writing rather than on what words they have read during Guided Reading. **The emphasis is still on high-frequency words, but select those that are irregularly spelled, particularly those misspelled in students' first-draft writing.** Many second-grade teachers begin their Word Walls with the words **they**, **said**, **was**, **have**, and **because**—words that most second graders can read but cannot spell. (Do not put high-frequency words that are easy to spell on a second-grade Word Wall unless you have second graders who still cannot spell **me**, **in**, **go**, etc.) Hard-to-spell high-frequency words are often on the first-grade Word Wall and also put on the second-grade Word Wall. Students who had a Word Wall in first grade often know which words are hard for them to spell, and they ask to have these words put on the Word Wall.

The Word Wall grows as the year goes on. Each week, write the words on sheets of colorful paper. Avoid dark colors on which letters won't show up! The words need to be large enough to be seen from anywhere in the room. If two or more words begin with the same letter in a parcular week, use a different paper color for each word. After writing each word with a thick, black permanent marker, cut around the letters to emphasize which letters go above and below the lines. Words are placed on the wall alphabetically, and the first words added are very different from each other. When words are added that are similar to ones already on the Word Wall, put them on different paper colors from the words with which they are usually confused.

Most teachers add five new words each week and do at least one daily activity in which students chant, cheer, and write the spellings of the words. The activity takes longer on the days that words are added because the teacher takes time to make sure that students associate meanings with the words and points out how the words are different from words with which they are often confused. Some teachers add the new words at the beginning of the week; others wait until the end of the week, keeping the words separate for a while. **Continue adding five new words each week. Practice the new words for a few days and spend the remaining days practicing words from previous weeks.**

Daily Word Wall Practice

1. Begin by giving each student a half sheet of handwriting paper that he numbers from 1 to 5.

2. Call out a word and use it in a sentence. As you call out each word, students locate the word on the wall and keep looking at it (**visual**). After you have said the word, have students cheer, clap, or snap the word. "T-H-E-Y—they!" (**auditory rhythmic**).

3. Have each student write the word on the line beside the number on his paper (**kinesthetic**). Write the word on the board or the overhead as students write it on their papers. This will emphasize the correct formation of the letters as students watch you and write.

4. Repeat the procedure for the four remaining words.

5. After all five words are looked at, cheered, and written, lead students to check the spellings by touching each letter as you say it. They can also "shape" each word and look at their handwriting by drawing around the shape of the word, noticing which letters go above and/or below the lines.

At right is what a student's paper would look like.

```
Mario
1. they
2. said
3. was
4. have
5. because
```

Selecting Word Wall Words

Besides the hard-to-spell high-frequency words, try to include the following:

- Example words for digraphs including **ch**, **kn**, **ph**, **qu**, and **wr**

- The less common **c /s/** and **g /j/** sounds

- The most common blends: **bl**, **br**, **cl**, **cr**, **dr**, **fl**, **fr**, **gr**, **pl**, **pr**, **sk**, **sl**, **sm**, **sn**, **sp**, **st**, and **tr**

- The most common vowel patterns:

    a crash, make, rain, played, car, saw, caught, black, made, mail, name, sale, small, than, thank, skate

    e went, eating, green, sister, new, best, tell, then

    i into, ride, right, girl, thing, write, kicked, line, nice, drink, will, trip

    o not, those, float, or, outside, boy, shook, school, how, slow, more, sports, stop, our, clock, found, joke, phone

    u bug, use, hurt, jump, junk, truck

    y why, very

- The most commonly written contractions: **can't**, **didn't**, **don't**, **it's**, **that's**, **they're**, **won't**

- Common homophones: **to/too/two**; **there/their/they're**; **right/write**; **one/won**; **new/knew**

- Example words with **s**, **ed**, and **ing** endings

Word Wall Words for Second Grade

Here is a Word Wall list for second grade that includes everything described in Selecting Word Wall Words (page 18). The boldfaced words below are often used on a first-grade Word Wall, but are included here because it takes some students two years to learn to spell these words automatically every time they write them. Many teachers underline or use a visual symbol beside words with spelling patterns that help students spell a lot of rhyming words. Common spelling patterns are underlined in the words below. This list also includes clue words in parentheses to help students distinguish between **homophones**, words that sound the same but have different spellings and meanings. Each clue should be mounted on the Word Wall next to the corresponding homophone.

120 High-Frequency Second-Grade Words

about	eating	**little**	right (wrong)	**thing**
after	every	**made**	**said**	those
again	**favorite**	mail	sale	**to**
are	first	**make**	**saw**	too (too late!)
beautiful	float	many	**school**	trip
because	found	more	shook	truck
before	friends	name	**sister**	two (2)
best	**girl**	**new** (old)	skate	use
black	green	**nice**	slow	**very**
boy	gym	**not**	small	wanted
brothers	**have**	**off**	snap	**was**
bug	**here**	one (1)	sometimes	**went**
can't	house	or	sports	were
car	**how**	other	stop	what
caught	hurt	our	**tell**	when
children	I	outside	than	where
city	into	**people**	thank	who
clock	it's	phone	that's	why
could	joke	played	their	will
crash	**jump**	**pretty**	**them**	with
crashes	junk	**quit**	then	won
didn't	kicked	**rain**	**there** (here)	**won't**
don't	knew	really	**they**	write
drink	line	**ride**	they're (they are)	writing

How the Word Wall Is Multilevel

Word Wall activities can meet the needs of a wide range of second-grade students because there are a variety of things to be learned. Most second-grade students can read these words but cannot spell them. Daily Word Wall practice provides a second opportunity for the students who did not learn to read these high-frequency words in first grade. Other students learn to spell them correctly and are reminded to do so when they write. The daily practice and the demand for the correct spelling of all Word Wall words when writing will eventually help students replace the automatic incorrect spellings with automatic correct spellings. For students who are already spelling all of these words correctly, the daily practice is a time when they can work on their handwriting—a skill that many second graders have not perfected.

Rounding Up the Rhymes

20–25 min.

Rounding Up the Rhymes is an easy activity for second-grade students, but it is fun! This activity is enormously popular with students. They enjoy chiming in on the rereading of the book and telling you the words that rhyme. Often, Rounding Up the Rhymes is a necessary activity for students who don't understand the concept of rhyme. Most students find this an easy task—but this was not always true in first grade! **This activity can follow the reading of any story, book, or poem that has a lot of rhyming words. The first, and often the second, reading of anything should focus on meaning and enjoyment.**

How I Spent My Summer Vacation by Mark Teague (Knopf Books for Young Readers, 1995)

This is the story of a boy who tells his class about his summer vacation. He claims that his parents sent him to visit an aunt out west where he was captured by cowboys and had many exciting adventures. What a fun book for students to listen to! What is real? What did Wallace make up and why? Students will add their tall tales to the adventures of Wallace! They love making up good stories and telling what could have happened to them.

The second or third reading of the book is an appropriate time to call students' attention to the rhyming words. As you read each page or two again, encourage students to listen for the rhymes as you say them. As students identify the rhyming words, write 10–12 pairs on index cards and put them in a pocket chart.

"When summer began I headed out west.

My parents had told me I needed a rest."

When students tell you that **west** and **rest** are the rhyming words, write those two words and continue reading. **Some of the rhyming pairs will have the same spelling patterns (west** and **rest) and some will not (crowd** and **loud).** When you are finished writing the rhyming words, have students help you discard rhyming pairs without the same spelling patterns. You will be left with the following:

| west | sit | say | hat | tricks |
| rest | quit | okay | that | sticks |

| land | day | eat | sight | day |
| cowhand | way | beat | fright | say |

| ground | display | buckaroo |
| around | away | too |

(Note: On the chart, the following words are crossed out: sit, say, quit, okay, land, day, eat, day, cowhand, way, beat, say, display, buckaroo, away, too.)

Finally, remind students that thinking of rhyming words can help them when they are reading and writing. Write a word that rhymes with some rounded-up rhymes and show it to students. Have them put the new word under the pair that will help them figure it out and use the rounded-up rhymes to decode the word.

"What if you were reading and came to this word?" Show **pound**. "What words in the pocket chart would help you read this word?" Yes, **ground** and **around** have the same spelling pattern and rhyme. Let's see . . . gr—**ound**, p—**ound**. That word is **pound**. They wanted a **pound** of meat."

Next, say a word they might need to write—but do not show it.

"What if you were writing and wanted to write the word **treat**? What words would help you write **treat** correctly? That's right. **Eat** and **beat** can help you write **treat**. Add **tr** to the spelling pattern **eat** and you have **treat**."

You may want to continue this for a few more words (**flight**, **tray**), especially if this is the first time you have rounded up the rhymes and transferred to reading and writing new words. For example, **sight** and **fright** will help students with **flight** and **say**, **okay**, **day**, and **way** will help them with **tray**.

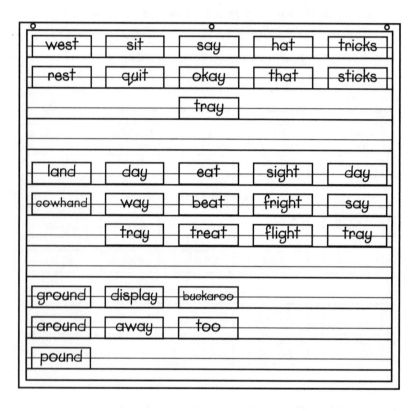

Any book or story with a lot of rhymes is a good candidate for a Rounding Up the Rhymes lesson. Many teachers tie in this activity with an author study of Dr. Seuss.

Additional Rhyming Books

Each Peach Pear Plum by Janet Ahlberg and Allan Ahlberg (Scholastic, 1978)

House Mouse, Senate Mouse by Peter W. Barnes and Cheryl Shaw Barnes (VSP Books, 1996)

How Many, How Many, How Many by Rick Walton (Candlewick Press, 1993)

The Library by Sarah Stewart (Farrar, Straus and Giroux, 1995)

Madeline by Ludwig Bemelmans (The Viking Press, 1939)

The Monster Book of ABC Sounds by Alan Snow (Dial, 1991)

My Teacher's My Friend by P. K. Hallinan (Ideals Publications, 2000)

Puffins Climb, Penguins Rhyme by Bruce McMillan (Gulliver Books, 1995)

The Rules by Marty Kelley (Knowledge Unlimited, 2000)

This Is the Sea That Feeds Us by Robert Baldwin (Dawn Publicatins, 1998)

This Is the Way We Go to School by Edith Baer (Scholastic, 1990)

Wild about Books by Judy Sierra (Knopf Books for Young Readers, 2004)

Woodrow, the White House Mouse by Peter W. Barnes and Cheryl Shaw Barnes (VSP Books, 1995)

How Rounding Up the Rhymes Is Multilevel

Rounding Up the Rhymes is a multilevel activity. Struggling readers and writers whose phonemic awareness is limited learn what rhymes are and how to distinguish rimes from beginning sounds. Other students, whose phonemic awareness is better developed, learn a lot of spelling patterns and learn that rhyming words often share the same spelling patterns. Our most advanced readers and writers become proficient with the strategy of using words they know to decode and spell unknown words. This proficiency shows in their increased reading fluency and the more-sophisticated nature of the invented spellings they write.

20–25 min.

Guess the Covered Word

When you read, you recognize most words immediately because you have seen and read them before. When you do see words that you have never encountered, you figure them out. **Many words can be figured out by thinking about what would make sense in the sentence and seeing if the letters in the word match what you are thinking of. The ability to use the consonants and the context of the sentence is called cross-checking, and it is an important decoding strategy.** Students must learn to do two things simultaneously: think about what would make sense and think about letters and sounds. Most students would prefer to do one, but not both. Thus, some students guess something that is sensible but ignore the letter sounds they know. Other students guess something that sounds right but makes no sense in the sentence.

For each Guess the Covered Word lesson, write sentences on the board or on chart paper, covering the word to be guessed with two sticky notes; one that covers all of the letters up to the first vowel and one that covers the rest of the word.

To help students cross-check meaning with sound, do the following:

- **First, have students guess the covered word with no letters showing. There are generally many possibilities for a word that will fit the context of the sentence.**

- **Next, pull off the first sticky note, revealing the letters up to the first vowel and limiting the possibilities.** Students may have to make additional guesses if none of the possibilities are correct.

- **Finally, show the whole word and help students confirm which guess makes sense and has the right letters.**

For the first lessons, cover only words with a single beginning letter and place the unknown word at the end of each sentence. After these first lessons, include words with letter combinations, such as **sh**, **br**, and so on, and place these words in various places in the sentences. When covering the words, tear the sticky notes so that word lengths are visible. **Word length, beginning letters, and what makes sense are powerful clues when guessing an unknown word.**

Start with a Guess the Covered Word lesson about yourself and let students make four guesses for the boldfaced word in each sentence. They will enjoy finding out more about their second-grade teacher. Remember to use real information about yourself!

Your Teacher

I drive a **Camry**.

I have two **daughters**.

I live in a **gray** house.

I like to **read**.

I like to **shop**.

Here are some sample lessons in which the covered words are boldfaced. Remember that using your students' names helps keep them engaged!

Playing

Demetri likes to play **baseball**.

Michelle likes to play **tag**.

Jack likes to play **football**.

Mrs. Daniel likes to play **cards**.

Alex likes to play with her **dog**.

Our Classroom

The **paper** is on a shelf.

Oliver's **jacket** is in the closet.

Madeline sits next to **Billy**.

Meghan's **backpack** is new.

The teacher has a big **desk**.

Pets

Maggie's favorite pet is her **hamster**.

Michael would like a **parrot**.

Uma likes her **goldfish**.

Chan likes his little **dachshund**.

Taylor likes his new **kitten**.

September

All students are **happy** to be in school.

They like to **shout** at recess.

Jessie has fun with her new **friends**.

Myong likes to **stroll** around the yard.

Simon likes to run on the **track**.

Demetri likes to play b⬚.

~~soccer~~ ~~football~~
~~sports~~ basketball
baseball

Michelle likes to play ⬚.

ball   tennis
sports   tag

- First, show students the sentences and tell them that they will read each sentence and guess what word is covered. Have students read the first sentence and guess what the covered word is.

- Next to the sentence, write each guess that makes sense (**soccer**, **football**, **sports**, **basketball**, **baseball**). If a guess does not make sense, explain why and do not write that guess.

- When you have written several guesses, remove the sticky note that covers the first letter or letters (**b**). Erase or cross out any guesses that do not begin with this letter and ask if there are any more guesses that make sense and start with **b**.

- If there are more guesses, write them. Be sure that all guesses both make sense and start correctly. Some students will guess anything that begins with **b**. Respond with something like, "**Bowling** does begin with **b**, but you don't play bowling; you bowl. **Bowling** does not make sense in this sentence."

- When you have written all guesses that make sense and begin correctly, uncover the word. See if the word is one that students guessed. If students have the correct guess, praise their efforts. If not, say, "That was a tough one!" and go on to the next sentence.

Go through the same steps for each sentence:

1. Read the sentence and write three or four guesses that make sense.

2. Uncover the letter or letters up to the first vowel. Erase or cross out any guesses that don't begin with the correct letter or letters.

3. Have students make more guesses that both make sense and begin with the correct letter or letters. Write these guesses. (This step is a must if students did not generate any guesses with the correct beginning sound.)

4. Uncover the whole word and see if any of their guesses are correct.

How Guess the Covered Word Is Multilevel

Guess the Covered Word is a multilevel activity because there are different things to be learned by different students. Struggling readers learn to use all of the letters up to the first vowel, not just the beginning letter. When meeting an unknown word in text, they also learn to think, "What makes sense? What letter(s) does it begin with?" These are important concepts to learn in order to become a good reader. Average readers who know how to use context and phonics clues become more automatic at doing this. Because of the use of interesting words, accelerated readers learn more sight vocabulary and become even better at decoding.

Making Words

20–25 min.

Making Words (Cunningham and Cunningham, 1992) is an exciting, high-energy activity. In this activity, students arrange letters to make words. Students begin by making little words using a few of the given letters and progress to bigger words. The final word includes all of the letters, and students are eager to discover the secret word. Making Words is an activity in which students learn how to look for patterns in words and how changing just one letter or its location in a word changes the whole word. The little bit of extra preparation needed for the lesson will yield *big* results as students delight in their abilities to create and manipulate words!

Making Cards and Word Holders

The letter cards used in this activity can be made easily with tagboard or index cards, black and red markers, and scissors. Make a set for each student and one for yourself. To make each letter card, cut a square from the tagboard or index card. Students' squares should be about $1\frac{1}{2}$" in size, and your cards should be larger because they will be displayed in a pocket chart. Print a lowercase consonant in the center of each card in black. Turn over each card and print each uppercase letter. Set apart vowels from consonants by printing vowels in red.

Student word holders can be made by cutting file folders into 2" x 12" strips. For each holder, fold about $\frac{1}{4}$" of a long side and tape the edges together to make a pocket. The letter cards can be tucked into the shallow fold to make words in the holder.

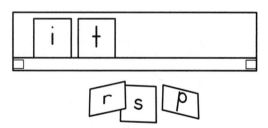

For most Making Words lessons, you will give each student 6–8 letters (including two vowels) to make 12–15 words. For the first lessons, however, limit the number of letters to five and include only one vowel. The five letters will make 8–10 words. The following pages present an example of a Making Words lesson that is first *prepared* and then *taught* in a second-grade classroom.

August/September

Preparing the Lesson

Imagine that you have decided that **trips** is the secret word and have pulled out (or made) the large letter cards for **trips**. Brainstorm a lot of little words that can be made from the letters in **trips**.

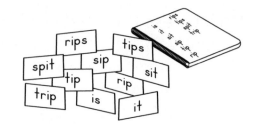

Decide which of the many words that you have brainstormed will make an easy and successful first lesson. Write these words on large index cards (for **trips**, write: **is**, **it**, **sit**, **sip**, **tip**, **rip**, **rips**, **tips/spit**, **trip**, and **trips**). Put the letter and words cards in a small envelope. On the outside of the envelope, write the words in the order that students will make them and the patterns for which you will have students sort (beginning **s** and **r** sounds, rhyming patterns **ip** and **it**, and plural words are all possibilities). You may even write two or three good transfer words (**kit**, **skit**, **chip**, and **ship**). Many second-grade workrooms have a communal box filled with hundreds of such envelopes. When you finish a lesson, add it to the box. You can make up a new lesson or, in a pinch, use one that was already planned.

Teaching a Sample Making Words Lesson

Step One: Making Words

1. To begin the lesson, place the large index cards with the letters **i**, **p**, **r**, **s**, and **t** in the bottom or top pocket of a pocket chart at the front of the classroom.

   Give each student a matching set of small letter cards and a word holder.

2. Pull each large card from the pocket chart and hold it up. Name the letter on each large card. Students hold up and name the letter on their matching cards.

   For these first lessons, you and your students show both the upper- and lowercase letters and discuss that the red letter is the vowel. Students count the letters and determine that they have four black letters (the consonants) and one red letter (the vowel) for a total of five letters.

3. Students get ready to make words by lining up their letters in front of their word holders.

   Tell students that every word must have a vowel. Today, each student has only one vowel—the red **i**. The **i** can be put in the word holder, and the student can work around it since every word will need it.

4. "The first word I want you to make has just two letters—**i** plus one more letter. The word is **is**. That is a word that most of us know. Everyone say **is**. Find the letter you need to add to **i** to spell **is**."

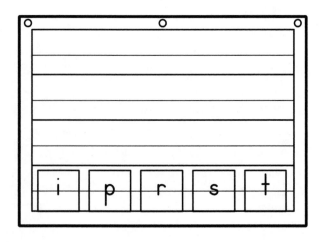

5. Watch as many students put **s** in their holders after **i**. Let one student who has made **is** correctly in her holder make it with the pocket-chart letters.

   "Good, **i** plus **s** spells **is**. Everyone check **is** in your holder. We are ready to make another word."

6. Place the index card that has **is** in the pocket chart. After each word is made with the big letters, place the index card with that word in the pocket chart. These index-card words will be sorted for patterns after all of the words are made.

7. Next, have students make the word **it**, listening to what sound is different and trying to find the letter that makes that sound.

8. Then, write **3** on the board for the next column. Tell students to add one letter to **it** to make the three-letter word **sit**. "I like to **sit** near my friend. Stretch out and listen to the beginning sound in **sit**. Put that letter in your holder before **it**."

   Let students who need to say the word out loud say it. Students will do this almost automatically if they need to hear the sounds in a word before finding the correct letters.

   As students attempt to make each word, select a student who has made that word correctly and send him to make the word with the large letters. Then, have everyone make the word before moving on to the next word. **It is very important for pacing—and to keep the lesson moving—not to wait for everyone to make the word before it is made with the big letters.** All students will have the word made after it is made with the big letters.

9. Next, tell students to change one letter in **sit** to spell **sip**. Give them a sentence for the new word. "I like to **sip** my drink." Have everyone say **sip**, stretching out the letters and listening for where they go. (Some students in second grade still need to hear themselves making the sounds so that they can transfer this ability to spelling words as they write.) Find someone with **sip** spelled correctly to make it with the big letters. Then, put the **sip** index card in the pocket chart and ask students to fix their words if needed.

10. Make the three-letter words **tip** and **rip**. Do not wait for everyone to spell each word correctly before sending someone to spell it with the big letters. But, make sure that everyone spells the word correctly before going to the next word. Place the index-card words in the pocket chart after each word is correctly made.

11. Write **4** on the board and show the class 4 fingers. Say to the class, "Now, we will make some four-letter words. If you add a letter to **rip**, you can make **rips**." This will not be difficult for most students.

   "Next, change **rips** to **tips**. Then, move around the letters in **tips** to make **spit**. We do not **spit** in school! Now, start over and make **trip**."

12. **Now is the time to tell students that when you plan the Making Words lesson, you always start with a secret word that can be made with all of the letters.** At the end of the lesson, ask:

   "Has anyone figured out the secret word—the one word that we can make using all of our letters?"

Tell students that some days, they will be able to figure out the word and other days, they won't, but that when they figure it out, they should keep it a secret until you ask the question.

"See if you can make a word that uses all of the letters."

Give students one minute to see if anyone can come up with the word. This is not likely if this is the very first lesson. **If anyone makes the word, send that student to the pocket chart and have her make the word. If not, tell students that the word is *trips*. Have a student make it with the big letters.** Be sure to have everyone make **trips** correctly in their holders.

To prepare for the sorting phase, have students close **trips** in their holders and direct their attention to the words in the pocket chart. **Once students get in the habit of Making Words, the making-words part should take no more than 10–15 minutes.** That leaves time at the end of each lesson for sorting words into patterns and using these patterns to read and spell a few new words. For the first several lessons, however, when students are learning how to manipulate the letters and make words, making the words might take longer! After five or six lessons, you should have the pace down for the lesson so that each lesson is completed in the 20–25 minutes allotted to this activity. **Keep the pace of an average student who is making the words. Never wait for your slowest student to make the word—let him make it while one student comes up to make it with the big letters and other students are checking.** When the activity is fast-paced, even your star students stay actively involved because they spell these words quickly.

Step Two: Sorting Words

Now, sort the words for patterns, which consist of beginning letters and rhymes at this time of year. Early in the year, direct the sort, but as the year goes on, students should start to look for patterns. Today, begin with **sit** and ask:

13. "Who can find another word that begins with **s**?" A student goes to the pocket chart and places **sip** under **sit**. Decide together that the words begin with the same letter and sound. The same procedure is used for **rip** and **rips**.

14. Next, go to the pocket chart and pull out the word **it**. "Now, I need someone who can find two words that end in **i-t**." A student places **sit** and **it** together in the pocket chart. Together, pronounce the two words and decide that they both end in **it** and rhyme.

15. The same procedure is followed for **i-p** (**sip**, **tip**, and **trip**).

Step Three: Transferring Words

Finally, when all of the words are sorted, tell students to pretend that it is writing time and that they need to spell some words that rhyme with some of the words that were made today. Have students use half sheets of paper to write the words. Say sentences that students might want to write that include rhyming words. Work together to decide with which words the new word in each sentence rhymes and to decide how to spell the word.

"Let's pretend that it is writing time. Kevin is writing about what he likes to eat for a snack, and he is trying to spell the word **chips**. Let's all say **chips** and stretch out the beginning letters. What two letters do you hear at the beginning of **chips**?"

Have students stretch out **chips** and listen for the beginning sound. Have them tell you what letters make that sound. When they tell you that **chips** begins with the **/ch/** sound, write **ch** on an index card and have students write **ch** on their papers.

Take the **ch** index card to the pocket chart. Hold it under each column of words (sorted under **it**, **sip**, and **rips**) as you lead students to chorally pronounce the words and decide if **chips** rhymes with them:

"**It**, **sit**, **spit**, **chips**?" Students should each show a thumbs-down.

"**Sip**, **tip**, **rip**, **trip**, **chips**?" Students should each show a thumbs-down.

"**Rips**, **tips**, **trips**, **chips**?" Students should each show a thumbs-up.

Finish writing **chips** on your index card by adding **ips** to **ch** and place **chips** in the pocket chart under **rips**, **tips**, and **trips**.

Make up sentences and use the same procedure to demonstrate how you use **it**, **sit**, and **spit** to spell **bit** and **slit** and **sip**, **tip**, and **rip** to spell **drip** and **slip**. Students' papers will have these five transfer words written on them: **chips**, **bit**, **slit**, **drip**, and **slip**.

A reproducible Making Words Take-Home Sheet can be found on page 164.

Making Words Lessons

One of the most difficult decisions teachers make is deciding when to move on to more difficult formats. Our observations tell us that some teachers move too fast, leaving behind a trail of struggling students while others, wanting everyone on board, never move! Of course, we must find a middle ground, which is easier said than done!

Most Making Words lessons in second grade have 6–8 letters, including two vowels. But students do need some practice with fewer letters and just one vowel so that they learn what the vowels are. Later lessons will have silent letters and letter combinations such as **ch**, **sh**, etc., but in the first lessons, students need to learn that if they stretch out words, they can hear a lot of the letters. This understanding really moves them along in their ability to spell words while writing.

For more lessons for second grade, see *Making Words: Second Grade* by Cunningham and Hall (Allyn & Bacon, 2009).

acorns

Letters: a o c n r s

Make: as, an, on, or, ran, can, car, cars, cans/scan, corn, acorns

Sort: c (can, car, cans, cars, corn) -an (an, ran, can, scan), -s pairs (can—cans, car—cars, acorn—acorns)

Transfer: van—vans, pans, plans

tracks

Letters: a c k r s t

Make: as, at, sat, cat, car, rat/tar, tack, rack, sack, stack/tacks, racks, track, tracks

Sort: c (cat, car), t (tar, tack, tacks), -at (at, sat, cat, rat), -ar (car, tar), -ack (tack, rack, sack, stack, track)

Transfer: scat, flat, star, smack

splash

Letters: a h l p s s

Make: as, has, sap, lap, ash, sash, lash, laps/slap, slaps, slash, splash

Sort: s (sap, sash), l (lap, lash, laps), sl (slap, slaps, slash), -ap (sap, lap, slap), -ash (ash, sash, lash, slash, splash)

Transfer: cash, crash, cap, trap

pumpkins

Letters: i u k m n p p s

Make: up, in, ink/kin, pin, pun, pup, pump, pink, mink, pumpkin, pumpkins

Sort: p (pin, pun, pump, pink, pumpkin), -in (in, kin, pin, pumpkin), -ink (ink, pink, mink)

Transfer: win, twin, wink, stink

apples
Letters: a e l p p s
Make: as, sap/spa, pal/lap, ape/pea, slap/pals, lapse, apple, apples
Sort: -ap (sap, lap, slap), -s pairs (pal—pals, apple—apples)
Transfer: clap, map—maps, trap—traps

blankets
Letters: a e b k l n s t
Make: sat, bat, bet, net, nest, best, last, tank, sank, bank, blank, blast, absent, basket, blanket, blankets
Sort: -ank (bank, sank, blank, tank), -et (bet, net), -est (best, nest), -at (sat, bat)
Transfer: jet, pest, chest, prank, plank

How Making Words Is Multilevel

Making Words is enormously popular with teachers and students. **Students love manipulating the letters, trying to figure out the secret word, and finding the patterns. Making Words works for students because (if your pacing is brisk!) students are all active, engaged, and successful.** Teachers like Making Words because students do, of course, but also because **they can see all levels of students growing in their word knowledge.** Every lesson begins with some short, easy words, and the teacher makes sure that everyone has each word made correctly after it is made with the pocket-chart letters. In early lessons, some strugglers are still learning to identify letters and are developing print concepts, such as first letter, last letter, beginning of word, and end of word. They are also still developing their phonemic awareness and learning that sounds in words can be manipulated. Making Words lessons let students succeed and practice on their own levels.

For most students who have not done this activity before second grade, Making Words is an activity through which **they are learning letter-sound relationships by stretching out words, hearing themselves making the sounds, and trying to match the sounds to a limited set of letters.** Some students can do this quite easily; others will learn. As students sort for beginning sounds and rhymes, they are beginning to understand how words work.

Every second-grade class, however, contains some students whose letter-sound knowledge is beyond simple beginning sounds and rhyming concepts. These students are always eager to figure out the secret word. As they try to do this, they are working with concepts beyond initial sound and rhyme. At the end of every Making Words lesson, it is important to show these students how the patterns in the words can help them figure out other words in their reading and writing. Students enter second grade with different levels of word knowledge. Making Words activities allow the range of students to make discoveries about words.

Applying Strategies When Reading and Writing

Some students read quite well without much help or guidance; other students need a lot of easy reading so that they can become fluent. Easy, predictable books found in most second-grade classrooms are good for increasing fluency. Rereading a familiar book also increases fluency. **Second-grade students need time to practice reading each day in order to gain fluency, especially if they are still reading word by word.** No matter what students' reading levels are, comprehension demands that they have some speed and accuracy so that they can concentrate on meaning rather than on decoding the words. **Set aside some time each day so that students can listen to you read and so that they can read and reread their favorite stories and books.**

When writing, some students need to be reminded to use the Word Wall. Others need to be reminded to write words that are not on the Word Wall by saying them slowly and writing the letters for the sounds they hear. Having students think about letters and sounds while they are reading and writing helps students apply what they are learning during the Working with Words Block to their daily reading and writing.

As you near the end of September, most students should have the level of phonemic awareness and letter-sound knowledge that they need to be successful in second grade. Many activities with students' names have been done, and you should know who is ready to use phonics and who is knowledgeable about beginning letters and sounds. It helps if you know who has not yet mastered these concepts so that you can continue to nudge them toward better understanding as you move into more-advanced decoding and spelling activities.

In August/September, **you started a Word Wall and let students know that these are important words that must be spelled correctly**—and that is easy because they can look at the words on the wall when needed. You also **had students make their own picture dictionaries**. (Maybe you even made one in a big-book size for yourself!) Now, students who want to spell words that are not high-frequency words can spell them correctly because **they will have personal dictionaries in which they keep their special words. Guess the Covered Word and Rounding Up the Rhymes help students develop and use their phonics knowledge**. These two multilevel activities help students **learn how words work when they are reading and writing**. For students to become good readers, they need to read, **so some time is set aside every day to read to students and to let them read self-selected materials on their own.**

October

Month at a Glance

October is here, and autumn is a part of the conversation and learning in many primary classrooms. Fall is different in various parts of the United States and Canada; in most places, there is a change in the weather and, therefore, a change in activities. Many areas continue the tradition of celebrating Halloween as a holiday at the end of the month. By this time in second grade, most classes have settled into a routine with some teacher-guided reading of basal readers or other books. Teachers also have a time each day to read aloud to students. Students should have time to practice new reading skills or strategies on their own levels during Self-Selected Reading time. Second-grade students also need time each day to write. During this daily writing time, each student writes about whatever she wants and shares it with the class on a weekly basis in an Author's Chair format. Students learn to take pieces from "sloppy copies" to "final drafts"—but not every piece. **These three components—Guided Reading, Self-Selected Reading, and Writing—form the core of a balanced literacy program and should occupy the majority of the instructional time in any second-grade classroom. The other component—learning to read and spell high-frequency words and to decode and spell a lot of less-frequent words—is the focus of this book.**

By the end of October, you will have **reviewed** the following:

- Use of the Word Wall as a visual cue for spelling high-frequency words

- Rounding Up the Rhymes to focus on and review vowel patterns

- Guess the Covered Word for cross-checking

- Making Words—a three-step, multilevel, hands-on activity:

    Step 1: Making words to develop phonemic awareness and to figure out how words work

    Step 2: Sorting words to help students look for patterns in beginning sounds, rhyming words, and endings

    Step 3: Transferring words—using patterns sorted for to write some new words

You will have **introduced** the following:

- On-the-Back activities that help transfer Word Wall words to a lot of other words by using the same spelling patterns in rhyming words

- Changing a Hen to a Fox to review beginning, middle (vowel), and ending sounds

- Coaching during independent and small-group reading time

30–35 min.

Working with Words Block

The Working with Words Block takes 30–35 minutes every day in second grade. The first 10 minutes should be spent practicing words on the Word Wall. That leaves 20–25 minutes for another activity—different activities can be done on different days. Three activities were introduced in the previous chapter—Guess the Covered Word, Rounding Up the Rhymes, and Making Words. This month, another activity—Changing a Hen to a Fox is added. This activity helps students develop word skills. These word skills are worthless, however, if students are not doing a lot of reading and writing. In fact, only if there are a lot of opportunities for students to apply their word skills in reading and writing will they get enough practice with words to become truly automatic and fluent in dealing with words.

As you move into October, the decoding and spelling focus is on learning more important high-frequency words. This is done with your Word Wall and some On-the-Back activities that move students forward in their word knowledge and help them use Word Wall words to write a lot of other words. You will continue Guess the Covered Word and Rounding Up the Rhymes activities. You will help students write some October theme words in their picture dictionaries and continue Making Words lessons so that your seven-year-olds experience some hands-on phonics instruction. You will also review beginning, middle (vowel), and ending sounds in Changing a Hen to a Fox. Learning about words can be fun!

10 min.

Word Wall

As outlined in the August/September chapter, **continue to add five new words each week, usually choosing the words on the second-grade list (page 19) that students misspell in their daily writing.** Remember that your students will need fall or Halloween words just this one month, so don't put them on the Word Wall. The Word Wall is the place for important words that students need every day throughout the year. Put seasonal words on a piece of chart paper or on a theme board or have students add them to their picture dictionaries. For more information on theme boards, see page 66.

Doing the Word Wall

Doing the Word Wall is not the same as having a Word Wall. Having a Word Wall might mean putting up all of these words somewhere in the room and telling students to use them. In this situation, struggling readers can't use them because they don't know them and don't know which is which! Doing a Word Wall means the following:

1. Being selective and stingy about what words you put on the wall, limiting the words to the words that students need a lot in writing

2. Adding the words gradually—five per week

3. Making the words accessible by putting them where all students can see them, writing them in big black letters, and using a variety of paper colors so that the commonly confused words (**for, from**; **that, them, they, this**; etc.) are on different colors

4. Practicing the words by chanting and writing them because struggling readers usually are not good visual learners and can't just look at and remember words

5. Doing a variety of review activities to provide enough practice that students read and spell the words instantly and automatically

6. Making sure that Word Wall words are spelled correctly in any student writing

Teachers who **do** Word Walls rather than **have** Word Walls report that all students write these critical words correctly during daily writing activities. **Each day, the Working with Words Block begins with the Word Wall** and doing five Word Wall words. If teachers have time, they do an On-the-Back activity. Starting in October, many second-grade classes need just five minutes to practice new Word Wall words or to review five words that are already on the Word Wall. The other five minutes can be used for an On-the-Back activity if the teacher is pacing everything just right.

On-the-Back Activity

Rhyming Words

Students do On-the-Back activities on the backs of the handwriting papers they used for Word Wall words. One of these activities is Rhyming Words, in which you choose a Word Wall word and use the spelling pattern to write other words. You might present the activity by saying, "All of the words on the Word Wall are important because we see them often when we read, and we need them when we write. Some of the words are also important because they help us spell a lot of other words." For this example, assume that **went** is already on the Word Wall.

"**Went** is one of these helpful words. Today, we will use it to spell other words. Write **went** on the backs of your Word Wall papers and underline the spelling pattern—**ent**. Under the word **went**, number your papers from 1 to 5."

1. "The first word we will write is **tent**. What if you were writing about the **tent** you slept in on your vacation? The spelling pattern **ent** in **went** would help you write **tent**. Everyone write **tent**."

2. "The second word we will write is **rent**. Tonight, we will **rent** a movie. Write **rent**."

3. "The next word is **sent**. My mother **sent** me to my room. Write **sent**."

4. "The fourth word is a name, **Brent**. **Brent** is a new student in our class. Write the letters you hear at the beginning of **Brent** and the spelling pattern that follows."

5. "The last word is **spent**. I **spent** all of my money. Write **spent**."

· ·

Check the five rhyming words with students, letting them correct the spellings of any words that need to be changed. Tell students that these are words they should be able to spell correctly since **went** is on the Word Wall and the **ent** spelling pattern is there for them to look at. Let them take home their papers and tell their families that they can spell these words. Parents like to know that you are teaching their children how to spell words.

This On-the-Back rhyming activity can be done with any Word Wall word that has a spelling pattern that will help students spell a lot of rhyming words. Be sure that each example for each sentence sounds like a sentence that one of your students might actually write. Doing this will achieve a maximum transfer to writing.

Here are some more words for Rhyming Words:

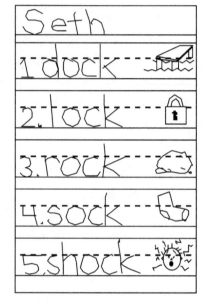

clock: dock, lock, rock, sock, shock

rain: pain, sprain, strain, train, brain

car: bar, far, star, jar, scar

stop: hop, chop, drop, shop, top

thank: bank, blank, shrank, tank, yank

boy: joy, Roy, soy, toy, Troy, enjoy

ride: hide, wide, side, bride, glide, slide

best: nest, rest, chest, vest, west

jump: bump, dump, pump, plump, thump

Each week when you introduce five new words, see which words have spelling patterns that can be used to make other words. Then, have students turn over their papers and do the Rhyming Words activity.

Having students draw simple pictures of Word Wall words and On-the-Back words helps ESL students and emergent readers learn the words.

Rounding Up the Rhymes

Remember to look for books with a lot of rhyming words when you are reading aloud to students or when they are reading selections during Guided Reading.

This Is the Pumpkin by Abby Levine (Albert Whitman & Co., 1997)

This story is written as a cumulative rhyme describing the activities of Max, his younger sister, and other students as they celebrate Halloween at school and while trick-or-treating at home. Students love this story and like to share how they will celebrate this day at school and at home, if they will celebrate it. **The first reading is for students to listen to the story and enjoy the book.**

The second and third readings of the book are appropriate times to call students' attention to the rhyming words. As you read each page, encourage students to listen for the rhymes. As students identify the rhyming words, write them on index cards and put them in a pocket chart.

"This is the costume, ghastly and **green**, that Max and his mom made for **Halloween**."

Students should tell you that **green** and **Halloween** are the rhyming words. Write those two words on index cards and put them in the pocket chart. (Instead of a pocket chart, some teachers use the board or a transparency.) The important thing is that once students hear the rhymes, they can then see the rhyming words. Some of the rhyming words will have the same spelling patterns (like **green** and **Halloween** and **block** and **o'clock**) and some will not (like **street** and **treat**). When you are finished writing the 10–12 rhyming pairs, the pocket chart will look like the one below.

green	block
Halloween	o'clock
west	parade
vest	lemonade
bright	stair
night	air
street	be
treat	me
beds	eye
heads	sky

Notice which rhyming pairs have the same spelling patterns and which do not. Have students help you discard rhyming pairs that do not have the same spelling patterns. If you use a pocket chart, remove these index cards and rip them up! This really makes the impression that if words have the same spelling pattern they are more helpful and if they don't have the same spelling pattern, they are not as useful. These pairs remain:

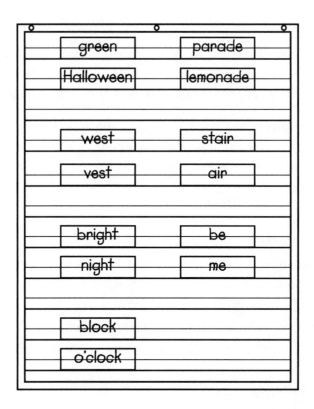

Finally, remind students that thinking of rhyming words can help them when they are reading and writing.

Write **between** on an index card. Then, show it to class but do not say it. "What if you were reading and came to this word? What words in the pocket chart would help you read this word? Yes, **green** and **Halloween** have the same spelling pattern and rhyme."

Model the separating of sounds so that students will understand what to do when they come to a word and they know the spelling pattern but not the word.

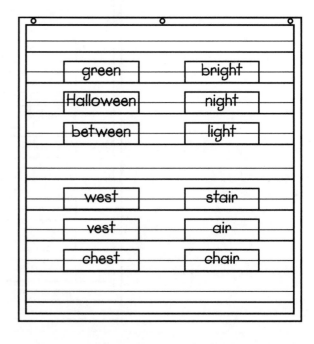

"Let's see . . . **be—tw—een**. The word is **between**. He was sitting **between** his two friends."

"What if you were writing and wanted to write **light**? What words would help you write **light** correctly? That's right, the spelling pattern in **bright** and **night** can help you write **light**. **Add l—** to the same spelling pattern **ight** and you have the word **light**."

You may want to continue this for a few more words (**chair** and **chest**), especially if your second graders need more practice transferring these words to reading and writing.

The Monster Book of ABC Sounds by Alan Snow (Dial, 1991)

Monsters are fun to read about and students like to pretend that they're real! Since this is an alphabet book, you can review letter sounds or finish your picture dictionaries with this book. After you read the story for enjoyment, you may want to make a chart of the monster sounds in alphabetical order. Then, round up the rhymes.

"The hide-and-seek game is about to **begin** . . .

The door is ajar and the rats go right **in**.

(This monster wasn't quite ready.)

Aaaaah!"

Have students tell you the rhyming words on this page (**begin** and **in**). Write them on index cards and place them in the pocket chart so that students can see the spelling patterns that are alike. Then, read the next two pages.

"Bb   A monster pops out from behind the door

Cc   while three cunning rats sneak a look 'neath the floor."

Have students tell you the two rhyming words (**door** and **floor**) on these two pages. Continue reading, identifying rhyming words, and writing those rhymes. Then, have students underline the rhyming parts of the words.

beg<u>in</u>	d<u>oor</u>	o'cl<u>ock</u>	w<u>et</u>	f<u>eet</u>	s<u>ong</u>	k<u>icks</u>	l<u>uck</u>
<u>in</u>	fl<u>oor</u>	sh<u>ock</u>	p<u>et</u>	<u>eat</u>	l<u>ong</u>	tr<u>icks</u>	d<u>uck</u>
m<u>ean</u>	th<u>irst</u>	b<u>oast</u>	gr<u>eat</u>				
s<u>een</u>	f<u>irst</u>	m<u>ost</u>	l<u>ate</u>				

Next, discard the words that do not have the same spelling patterns. These words remain:

beg<u>in</u>	d<u>oor</u>	o'cl<u>ock</u>	w<u>et</u>		s<u>ong</u>	k<u>icks</u>	l<u>uck</u>
<u>in</u>	fl<u>oor</u>	sh<u>ock</u>	p<u>et</u>		l<u>ong</u>	tr<u>icks</u>	d<u>uck</u>
	th<u>irst</u>						
	f<u>irst</u>						

Remind students that thinking of rhyming words can help them when they are reading and writing. "What if you were reading and came to the word **strong**? What two words would help you figure out that word? Right! The pattern in **song** and **long** will help you read **strong**. What if you were writing and wanted to write **stuck**? What spelling pattern would help you? That's right. **Uck** would help you, because **stuck** rhymes with **luck** and **duck**. Stretch it out: **st—uck**. Write **s-t** and the **uck** spelling pattern."

Do this activity again using two more transfer words like **bricks** and **knock**.

beg<u>in</u>	d<u>oor</u>	o'cl<u>ock</u>	w<u>et</u>		<u>song</u>	k<u>icks</u>	l<u>uck</u>
<u>in</u>	fl<u>oor</u>	sh<u>ock</u>	p<u>et</u>		l<u>ong</u>	tr<u>icks</u>	d<u>uck</u>
		kn<u>ock</u>			str<u>ong</u>	br<u>icks</u>	st<u>uck</u>

th<u>irst</u>
f<u>irst</u>

Come with Me on Halloween by Linda Hoffman Kimball (Albert Whitman & Co., 2005)

Read this book about a boy and his father who set out to go trick-or-treating on Halloween night. Are students surprised by the ending and who is scared? Read the book again and round up the rhymes, writing the rhyming words on index cards and putting them in a pocket chart. This is a little tricky because sometimes there are three rhyming words and the rhyming words are not always on the same pages. Sometimes, you need to read just one page and sometimes, you need to read two or three pages to find all of the rhyming words. When you finish rounding up the rhymes, the pocket chart should look like this:

flicker	right	howling	tight	sputter	chandelier
snicker	night	yowling	delight	flutter	near
bicker		prowling			

untangling	jiggle	creaking	team	dancing	staring
jangling	wiggle	peeking	scream	entrancing	glaring
		shrieking		prancing	daring

Then, have students underline the rhyming parts of the words:

fl<u>icker</u>	r<u>ight</u>	h<u>owling</u>	t<u>ight</u>	sp<u>utter</u>	chandel<u>ier</u>
sn<u>icker</u>	n<u>ight</u>	y<u>owling</u>	del<u>ight</u>	fl<u>utter</u>	n<u>ear</u>
b<u>icker</u>		pr<u>owling</u>			

unt<u>angling</u>	j<u>iggle</u>	cr<u>eaking</u>	t<u>eam</u>	d<u>ancing</u>	st<u>aring</u>
j<u>angling</u>	w<u>iggle</u>	p<u>eeking</u>	scr<u>eam</u>	entr<u>ancing</u>	gl<u>aring</u>
		shr<u>ieking</u>		pr<u>ancing</u>	d<u>aring</u>

Then, discard the rhyming pairs that do not have the same spelling patterns.

fl<u>icker</u>	r<u>ight</u>	h<u>owling</u>	t<u>ight</u>	sp<u>utter</u>
sn<u>icker</u>	n<u>ight</u>	y<u>owling</u>	del<u>ight</u>	fl<u>utter</u>
b<u>icker</u>		pr<u>owling</u>		

unt<u>angling</u>	j<u>iggle</u>	team	d<u>ancing</u>	st<u>aring</u>
j<u>angling</u>	w<u>iggle</u>	scr<u>eam</u>	entr<u>ancing</u>	gl<u>aring</u>
			pr<u>ancing</u>	d<u>aring</u>

Finally, have students read and write some transfer words.

fl<u>icker</u>	r<u>ight</u>	h<u>owling</u>	t<u>ight</u>	sp<u>utter</u>
sn<u>icker</u>	n<u>ight</u>	y<u>owling</u>	del<u>ight</u>	fl<u>utter</u>
b<u>icker</u>	s<u>ight</u>	pr<u>owling</u>	m<u>ight</u>	cl<u>utter</u>
tr<u>icker</u>		gr<u>owling</u>		

unt<u>angling</u>	j<u>iggle</u>	team	d<u>ancing</u>	st<u>aring</u>
j<u>angling</u>	w<u>iggle</u>	scr<u>eam</u>	entr<u>ancing</u>	gl<u>aring</u>
d<u>angling</u>		str<u>eam</u>	pr<u>ancing</u>	d<u>aring</u>

The Runaway Pumpkin by Kevin Lewis (Orchard, 2003)

Read the book and enjoy the story with your students. (To save time later and make Rounding Up the Rhymes an easier task, mark the pages that you want to reread.) Then, read the book again and round up the rhymes. During the second reading, you will notice that **round**, **ground**, and **sound** and **thumpkin**, **bumpkin**, and **pumpkin** are repeated four times. Write each set only once. At the end of the second reading, the pocket chart will look like this:

hill	fine	seen	them	faster	round
chill	vine	Halloween	stem	disaster	ground
Lil					sound

thumpkin	eye	coop	sped	plowed	up
bumpkin	pie	soup	bread	crowd	sup
pumpkin	sty	loop	head	proud	
			bed		

··

Next, have students underline the rhyming parts of the words.

hill	fine	seen	them	faster	round
chill	vine	Halloween	stem	disaster	ground
Lil					sound

thumpkin	eye	coop	sped	plowed	up
bumpkin	pie	soup	bread	crowd	sup
pumpkin	sty	loop	head	proud	
			bed		

Then, discard the words that do not have the same spelling patterns.

hill	fine	seen	them	faster	round
chill	vine	Halloween	stem	disaster	ground
					sound

thumpkin	coop	sped	bread	up
bumpkin	loop	bed	head	sup
pumpkin				

Finally, have students read and write some transfer words.

hill	fine	seen	them	faster	round
chill	vine	Halloween	stem	disaster	ground
spill	twine	teen	gem	plaster	sound
					found

thumpkin	coop	sped	bread	up
bumpkin	loop	bed	head	sup
pumpkin	droop	sled	dread	pup

Additional Rhyming Books

For October there are many rhyming books with a holiday theme, but it is fine to use any rhyming book. Just remember that if there are a lot of rhyming words in the book, choose only 10–12 pairs and round up the rhymes. Here are some more books you could use this month.

Jungle Halloween by Maryann Cocca-Leffler (Albert Whitman & Co., 2000)

More Parts by Tedd Arnold (Dial, 2001)

Parts by Tedd Arnold (Dial, 1997)

The Shape of Things by Dayle Ann Dodds (Candlewick Press, 1994)

Guess the Covered Word

20–25 min.

Some students never become really good at putting together sounds to decode words, but students can figure out most words by looking at the beginning letters and the lengths of the word and thinking about what words would make sense. Have you noticed your students saying, "This word couldn't be **peanut butter**. That is two words. Besides, this word is short. It has to be a short word like **pear** or **pie**." This is the cross-checking ability that Guess the Covered Word helps students develop. You can do Guess the Covered Word lessons with themes you are studying or books you are reading. **This month, the covered word can be anywhere in the sentence and can begin with two- and three-letter clusters, not just one-letter sounds.**

October

The **leaves** are turning colors.

The nights are getting **longer**.

The days are getting **cooler**.

Children want Halloween to come.

They will dress in funny **clothes**.

Halloween

Rosa went to a **party**.

The **clothes** people wore were funny.

At the party, someone wore a **black** mask.

The **princess** was the best costume.

The **dragon** was the scariest costume.

Favorite Foods

Kevin likes to eat **cheese** sandwiches.

Sadaf likes to eat **pretzels** for a snack.

Fried **chicken** is José's favorite food.

Jasmin likes **crackers**.

Suzanne likes **broccoli**.

Marie likes to eat **brownies**.

The Monster Book of ABC Sounds*

The monster hides behind a **small** door.

The monster likes to **play**.

One monster eats **bread**.

One monster is **thirsty**.

The monsters and the rats have a **great** time!

---

* *The Monster Book of ABC Sounds* by Alan Snow (Dial, 1991)

20–25 min.

Making Words

Making Words lessons are usually done twice a week while the other activities are done once a week. In these lessons, second-grade students learn about letter sounds and vowel patterns by manipulating the letters and Making Words. They become better at detecting patterns during the sort step. This month, continue to sort for beginning sounds and short vowel patterns, include one r-controlled vowel pattern, **ar**, in the **rabbit** lesson. Students learn to transfer what they learn to their reading and writing when we prompt them during the transfer step.

Making Words Lessons

ghost
Letters: o g h s t
Make: to, so, go, got, hot, hog, hogs, host/shot, ghost
Sort: g (go, got), h (hot, hog, hogs, host), -ot (got, hot, shot), -ost (host, ghost)
Transfer: pot, rot, post, most

rabbits
Letters: a i b b r s t
Make: at, sat, rat, bat, bar, tar, star, stir, stair, rabbit, rabbits
Sort: b (bat, bar), st (star, stir, stair), -at (at, sat, rat, bat)
Transfer: that, flat, jar, scar

contests
Letters: e o c n s s t t
Make: on, con, cot, not, net, set, sent, nest, test, tent, tents, tests, contest, contests
Sort: -est (nest, test, contest), -on (on, con), -et (net, set), -ent (sent, tent)
Transfer: vest, chest, wet, dent, spent

stopped
Letters: e o d p p s t
Make: set, pet, pot/top, pop, pep, step, stop/spot, pots, pets/pest, stopped
Sort: -op (top, pop, stop), -et (pet, set), -ot (pot, spot)
Transfer: vet, mop, drop, flop, chop, drop

chipmunks
Letters: i u c h k m n p s
Make: in, up, cup, pin/nip, chip, chin/inch, much, munch, punch, pinch, chipmunk, chipmunks
Sort: -in (in, pin, chin), -unch (munch, punch), -inch (inch, pinch), -ip (nip, chip), -up (up, cup)
Transfer: thin, spin, bunch, crunch, flip, trip

children
Letters: e i c d h l n r
Make: in, Ed, red, rid, hid, lid, led, Ned/den/end, her, herd, chin/inch, child, children
Sort: -ed (Ed, red, led, Ned), -id (rid, hid, lid), -in (in, chin)
Transfer: fed, sled, kid, skid, win, skin

bathtubs
Letters: a u b b h s t t
Make: as, us, bus/sub, tub, tab/bat, sat, hat, hut, but, shut, that, bath, bathtub, bathtubs
Sort: -at (bat, sat, hat, that), -us (us, bus), -ut (but, hut, shut), -ub (tub, sub, bathtub)
Transfer: chat, scat, nut, club, scrub

giants
Letters: a i g n s t
Make: in, it, at, an, ant/tan, tin, sit, sat, ants/tans, tins, gain, stain, giant, giants
Sort: -at (at, sat), -an (an, tan), -in (in, tin), plurals (ants, tans, tins, giants)
Transfer: flat, plan, scan, win, spin, skin

20–25 min.

Changing a Hen to a Fox

Teachers want to know how much their students know about letter sounds. They watch them during Making Words, but there is no number of right or wrong words recorded— and there shouldn't be! Sometimes, however, teachers want to see how well their students do on paper. Changing a Hen to a Fox allows teachers to do this.

Write key words on the board:

cat   hen   pig   fox   bug

Ask students to say these words and call students' attention to the fact that they can hear the beginning, middle, and ending sounds in each of these words. Next, ask students, "Can you change a hen to a fox?" Tell students that if they follow your directions and think about letters and sounds, they will be able to do this.

"Write **hen**." (This is already on the board, so all students can easily write **hen**.)

"Now, change **hen** to **pen**. A pen is something with which you write." (Give students one minute or less to do this one-letter change.)

"Then, change **pen** to **pet**. I have a pet dog." (Give students one minute or less to do this.)

"Can you change **pet** to **pit**? A peach has a pit inside."

"Then, change **pit** to **sit**. I like to sit near the window."

"Next, change **sit** to **six**. In first grade, you were six years old."

"Then, change **six** to **fix**. Who will fix the broken chair?"

"Last, change **fix** to **fox**. A fox was in the woods."

"If you have made these changes correctly, you have changed a **hen** to a **fox**!"

Students can correct their papers with you. This activity will show you what each student knows about beginning, ending, and vowel sounds.

Here are seven other lessons you can do with your class this month:

> - pig, rig, rid, rib, rob, Bob, box, fox
> - bug, dug, dig, pig, pin, pen, ten, hen
> - pig, big, wig, win, fin, fit, fat, cat
> - cat, bat, hat, rat, pat, pet, pen, hen
> - fox, box, bop, top, mop, map, mat, cat
> - bug, hug, dug, dig, big, bag, bat, cat
> - cat, hat, rat, rag, bag, big, dig, pig

How Changing a Hen to a Fox Is Multilevel

Changing a Hen to a Fox is a review activity for beginning, middle (vowel), and ending sounds. The thought process that each student goes through in order to complete this activity is the multilevel part. Your more-advanced readers and writers may write these words quickly. For these students, it is a time to recall and write words automatically using their word knowledge. Other students, who are not as far along in their word knowledge, learn to say each word slowly and listen for the sounds. Then, they learn to write the letters that represent those sounds. Your struggling students are not only listening to the sounds but are also matching them to the sounds that they hear in key words, then writing the letters on their papers. What students need to be successful depends on what they know and the opportunities you give them. Changing a Hen to a Fox is a wonderful way to review letter-sound knowledge. This activity also lets students with a wide range of abilities use what they know to write one-syllable words.

Applying Strategies When Reading and Writing

Daily reading and writing continues with the hope that the strategies taught during the Working with Words Block will be used during the other three blocks. Some second-grade students know a lot more about letters, sounds, and spelling patterns than they use when they are reading and writing. The work you are doing with words and phonics is useful only if students use it while they are actually reading and writing.

Coaching during Reading

If you have students who stop when they come to a word they don't know, coaching them will help. **Your instruction is more effective if you lead students through the steps to reading a new word at the moment they encounter the word.** Here are some coaching suggestions for when a student does not know a word:

1. Put your finger on the word and say all of the letters.

2. Use the letters and picture clues.

3. Try to pronounce the word by seeing if it has a spelling pattern or rhyme that you know.

4. Keep your finger on the word and read the other words in the sentence to see if what you think the word is makes sense.

5. If it doesn't make sense, go back to the word and think about what word would make sense and has those letters.

A good reader looks at all of the letters in a word that he is trying to read. A student who is struggling with reading tends to look quickly at the word, and if he doesn't instantly recognize it, he may either wait for someone to tell him the word or guess the word. Asking him to say all of the letters forces him to look at all of the letters. Sometimes after saying all of the letters, the student may say the word correctly!

By watching students as they do the activities in the Working with Words Block and observing and assessing students one-on-one during the Self-Selected Reading and Writing Blocks, you will notice the progress that students are making.

- Some students do these tasks easily.

- Be sure that the more-advanced students are transferring this learning from the Working with Words Block to reading and writing.

- Other students can do the tasks but work hard to do so.

- Still other students need help to accomplish these tasks. Continue to focus on these students.

As the month ends with a spooky holiday, teachers see that students are having fun and it becomes a treat to teach phonics. Words are no longer tricking their students!

November

Month at a Glance

November is a good time to be thankful for the success that your students are making in school this year. The classroom routines are well established, and students are on their way to learning more about how words work. In the United States, Thanksgiving is just around the corner. Many second graders know about this holiday from kindergarten and first grade as family Thanksgiving traditions. Students like to talk about why the Pilgrims were thankful on that first U.S. Thanksgiving in Plymouth, Massachusetts. Many seasonal words can be added to students' picture dictionaries or a theme board. Because students will use these words only this month, teachers have bulletin boards or theme boards to capture some key ideas and words that can be used when writing about Thanksgiving.

Teachers have several reasons to celebrate. In addition to their families and friends, they are thankful for their students who keep them busy but whom they think are wonderful. These same students have many reasons why they are thankful. These reasons usually revolve around their food, their families, their homes, their friends, and all of the things they enjoy! Both teachers and parents are pleased that the children are learning how to read and write—a blessing for which all of us should be thankful!

By the end of November, you will have **reviewed** the following:

- On-the-Back activities that help transfer Word Wall words to other words by adding endings to Word Wall words
- Rounding Up the Rhymes lessons that help students review beginning sounds and use the spelling patterns in rhyming words to spell a lot of new words
- Guess the Covered Word with blends and digraphs at the beginnings of the covered words and with the covered words in the middles or at the ends of the sentences

By the end of November, you will have **introduced** the following:

- Making Words activities with seasonal words and more letters and vowels
- How a lot of easy reading builds speed and fluency
- Reading/Writing Rhymes as another way to work on short vowel patterns

Word Wall

10 min.

In November, **continue adding five words to the wall each week**, choosing words from the second-grade high-frequency word list (page 19). Choose words that many students are misspelling during their daily writing. Each week, continue calling out the new words for a few days and reviewing five words already on the wall for the remaining days. Whether new or review words, have students chant, cheer, and write the words. As you write them, model correct handwriting for all of the letters in the words. Students should watch and form each letter in each word correctly. Then, have students self-correct their papers.

Theme Board

November is another month in which a lot of seasonal words enter students' writing. They want to tell you things for which they are thankful. They want to tell you what they know about Thanksgiving. These words will be used in students' writing only in November, so they do not go on the Word Wall; Word Wall words are words that they need all year. But, the words can go on a theme board or a sheet of chart paper that you can take down when December begins. Some November words might be **thankful, Pilgrims, Mayflower, Plymouth, turkey, harvest,** and **feast**.

On-the-Back Activities

Adding Endings to Words

An On-the-Back activity you may want to introduce this month is Adding Endings to Words. When you finish your daily Word Wall practice, have students turn over their Word Wall papers and do this activity on the backs of their papers. **On-the-Back activities are designed to help students learn that some of the words on the wall can help them spell a lot of other words.** When beginning this activity, you might say:

> "All of the words on the Word Wall are important because we see them often in the books we read and because we need them when we write. But, some words are important in other ways. If you know word endings, some of the words on the wall will help you spell a lot of other words that are longer but use the base word. **Want** is one of these helpful words. We will practice using Word Wall words when they have endings added to them. Turn over your paper. Write the word **want**. Number your paper from 1 to 3."

1. "The first word is **wants**. You might be writing about how your brother **wants** a dog. Let's say **wants** slowly and listen for the sound at the end. Yes, **wants** has **s** at the end. Add **s** to **want** and you have the word **wants**."

Continue the On-the-Back lesson by giving students possible scenarios in which they would need to use endings to help them spell other words.

2. "What if you were writing about the football game and how you **wanted** your team to win? Say **wanted** slowly. What letters would you add to **want** to spell **wanted**? Yes, add **ed** to **want** and spell **wanted**. Write **wanted** on the next line."

3. "What if you were writing about yourself and how you were **wanting** to make friends with the new girl in the class. What would you add to **want** to write **wanting**? Yes, add **ing** to **want** to spell **wanting**. Write **wanting** on the third line."

After having students write **want** with the different endings (**s**, **ed**, and **ing**) on the backs of their Word Wall papers, have students check them by reading and spelling them together. Some other second-grade Word Wall words with which you can do this activity are the following:

Sample On-the-Back Lessons with Word Endings

crash: crashes, crashing, crashed

drink: drinks, drinking, drinker

eat: eats, eating, eater

float: floats, floater, floating, floated

jump: jumps, jumper, jumping, jumped

kick: kicks, kicking, kicked, kicker

mail: mails, mailing, mailer, mailed

play: plays, player, playing, played

Rhyming Words

You now have two On-the-Back activities to use: Rhyming Words and Adding Endings to Words. Which activity you choose depends on what words you are introducing or practicing each day.

Sample On-the-Back Lessons for Rhyming Words

crash: cash, dash, gash, sash, stash

drink: pink, sink, rink, stink, shrink

eat: beat, heat, meat, treat, wheat

float: boat, coat, oat, bloat, throat

jump: bump, dump, pump, stump, plump

kick: Rick, sick, stick, flick, trick

mail: bail, tail, trail, rail, snail

play: day, May, hay, pray, stray

20–25 min.

Rounding Up the Rhymes

There are many books with a Thanksgiving theme that you can use for Rounding Up the Rhymes in November.

Today Is Thanksgiving! by P. K. Hallinan (Ideals Children's Books, 2001)

Read this book about Thanksgiving, family, and memories. Then, read some of the pages again and round up the rhymes on those pages. Do not find the rhymes in the whole book because there are too many rhymes. Read a few pages and write these pairs on index cards:

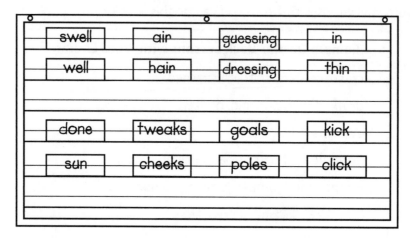

Next, have students underline the rhyming parts of the words.

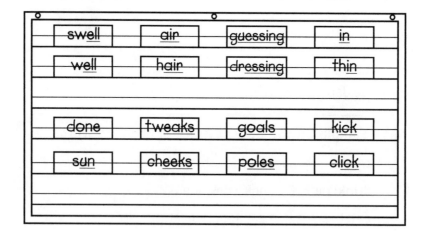

Then, discard the rhyming pairs that do not have the same spelling patterns.

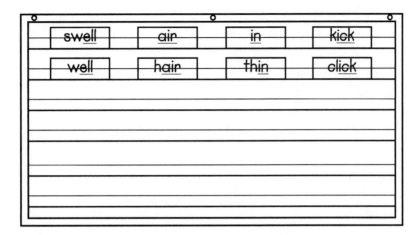

Finally, have students read and write some transfer words.

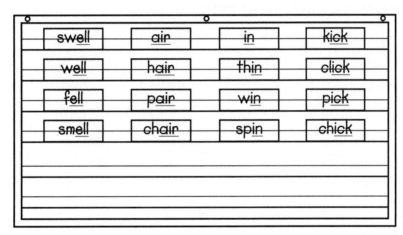

Shiver Me Letters: A Pirate ABC by June Sobel (Harcourt Children's Books, 2006)

Read this alphabet book to students and enjoy a pirate adventure. Then, round up the rhymes.

rough	west	ear	gold	appeared	ocean
tough	quest	cheer	old	beard	commotion
nest	bunch	sword	net	hot	thanks
rest	lunch	aboard	wet	spot	planks

Next, have students underline the rhyming parts of the words.

| r<u>ough</u> | w<u>est</u> | <u>ear</u> | g<u>old</u> | app<u>eared</u> | oc<u>ean</u> |
| t<u>ough</u> | qu<u>est</u> | ch<u>eer</u> | <u>old</u> | b<u>eard</u> | comm<u>otion</u> |

| n<u>est</u> | b<u>unch</u> | sw<u>ord</u> | n<u>et</u> | h<u>ot</u> | th<u>anks</u> |
| r<u>est</u> | l<u>unch</u> | ab<u>oard</u> | w<u>et</u> | sp<u>ot</u> | pl<u>anks</u> |

Then, discard the rhyming pairs that do not have the same spelling patterns.

| r<u>ough</u> | w<u>est</u> | | g<u>old</u> | |
| t<u>ough</u> | qu<u>est</u> | | <u>old</u> | |

| n<u>est</u> | b<u>unch</u> | | n<u>et</u> | h<u>ot</u> | th<u>anks</u> |
| r<u>est</u> | l<u>unch</u> | | w<u>et</u> | sp<u>ot</u> | pl<u>anks</u> |

Finally, have students read and write some transfer words.

r<u>ough</u>	w<u>est</u>		g<u>old</u>
t<u>ough</u>	qu<u>est</u>		<u>old</u>
en<u>ough</u>	cr<u>est</u>		t<u>old</u>

n<u>est</u>	b<u>unch</u>		n<u>et</u>	h<u>ot</u>	th<u>anks</u>
r<u>est</u>	l<u>unch</u>		w<u>et</u>	sp<u>ot</u>	pl<u>anks</u>
v<u>est</u>	m<u>unch</u>		j<u>et</u>	pl<u>ot</u>	bl<u>anks</u>

Additional Rhyming Books

Other rhyming books you could use this month for Rounding Up the Rhymes include:

'Twas the Day After Thanksgiving by Mavis Smith (Little Simon, 2002)

'Twas the Night Before Thanksgiving by Dav Pilkey (Scholastic, 1990)

A Rainbow of Friends by P. K. Hallinan (Ideals Publications, 2001)

Guess the Covered Word

20–25 min. On some days, continue to use your time after Word Wall for Guess the Covered Word lessons. Some students never become really good at putting together sounds to decode words, but students can figure out most words by looking at the beginning letters and the lengths of the words and thinking about what words would make sense. **Guess the Covered Word helps students develop this cross-checking ability.** For some students, this is their most successful decoding activity. Below are a few possible lessons. **Remember to use the names of your students and relate your sentences to what interests them.**

November

In November, Mike watches **football**.

Heidi wears a **sweater**.

Our class learns a lot about **Thanksgiving**.

Antoinette is baking a **pumpkin** pie.

Amy will **bring** the fruit.

Who will cook the **feast**?

Those Can-Do Pigs*

Those Can-Do pigs can repair **chairs**.

Can-Do pigs like to make **music**.

Other Can-Do pigs can fly like **birds**.

A **broom** helps those pigs clean.

Snacks are what Can-Do pigs like to eat.

A Can-Do pig can be a good **friend**.

The First Thanksgiving

The **Pilgrims** came to America on a ship.

It was a long, hard **voyage** across the ocean.

Many people were **crowded** on the ship.

The Pilgrims **planted** their own food.

Native Americans helped them plant **food**.

They gave thanks for their **blessings**.

Math

We learn about **shapes** in math.

Sometimes, **problems** are hard to do.

Often we make **graphs**.

Flash **cards** help us learn our facts.

We have to **practice** addition facts.

We also practice **subtraction** facts.

Those Can-Do Pigs by David McPhail (Dutton Juvenile, 1996)

20–25 min.

Making Words

Once you have done several easy Making Words lessons, you are ready to do lessons that sort for beginning sounds, silent letters, different spelling patterns, and endings. **Sorting for all of these things helps students to see how words work and how to use letter sounds, spelling patterns, and endings when they are writing.** Following are eight lessons for November. These secret words fit into a November theme. You may want to sort for specific phonics elements that your students are learning. For additional Making Words lists and suggestions, refer to *Making Words Second Grade* by Cunningham and Hall (Allyn & Bacon, 2009).

Making Words Lessons

November
Letters: e e o b m n r v
Make: be, me, men, Ben, mob, rob, robe/bore, more, been, November
Sort: -en (men, Ben), -ob (mob, Rob), -ore (bore, more)
Transfer: when, snore, cob, throb

turkeys
Letters: e u k r s t y
Make: us, use, set, yet, key, rut, ruts/rust, keys, true, rusty, turkey, turkeys
Sort: plurals (ruts, keys, turkeys), -et (set, yet)
Transfer: pet, vet, nets, jets

Pilgrims
Letters: i i g l m p r s
Make: is, lip, sip, rip, rig, pig, pigs, lips/slip, grip, girl, girls, Pilgrim, Pilgrims
Sort: r (rip, rig), p (pig, pigs, Pilgrim, Pilgrims), -ip (lip, sip, rip, slip, grip), -ig (rig, pig), plurals (pigs, lips, girls, Pilgrims)
Transfer: ship, trip, dig, twig

vegetables
Letters: a e e e b g l s t v
Make: at, bat/tab, gab/bag, sag, sat, set, vet, leg, beg, beat, seat, table, vegetable, vegetables
Sort: b (bat, bag, beg, beat), s (sag, sat, set, seat), t (tab, table), -at (at, bat, sat), -ag (bag, sag), -ab (tab, gab), -et (set, vet), -eg (leg, beg), -eat (beat, seat)
Transfer: flag, grab, peg, yet

potatoes

Letters: a e o o p t t s

Make: as, at, to, tot, pot, pat, pet, set, sat, stop/post, paste, taste, teapot, potato, potatoes

Sort: t (to, tot, taste, teapot), p (pot, pat, pet, post, paste, potato, potatoes), -at (at, pat, sat), -ot (tot, pot, teapot), -et (pet, set), -aste (paste, taste)

Transfer: hot, knot, wet, waste

Mayflower

Letters: a e o f l m r w y

Make: am, ram, yam/may, ray, way, lay, row, mow, low, flow, fray, flower, Mayflower

Sort: m (may, mow, Mayflower), fl (flow, flower), -am (am, ram, yam), -ay (may, ray, way, lay, fray), -ow (row, mow, low, flow)

Transfer: slam, tray, clay, slow

Thanksgiving

Letters: a i i g g h k n n s t v

Make: an, at, it, in, tin, tan/ant, van, vain, gain, sank, tank, thank, Thanksgiving

Sort: -in (in, tin), -an (an, tan, van), -ain (vain, gain), -ank (sank, tank, thank)

Transfer: plan, stain, plain, Frank

dinner

Letters: e i d n n r

Make: in, inn, end/Ned/den, die, red, rid, ride, rind, dine, nine, diner, dinner

Sort: d (den, die, dine, diner, dinner), r (red, rid, ride, rind), homophones (in—inn), -ed (Ned, red), -ine (dine, nine)

Transfer: grin, Ted, shed, pine, spine

20–25 min.

Reading/Writing Rhymes

Reading/Writing Rhymes is another activity that helps students learn to use patterns to decode and spell hundreds of words. In addition, all initial sounds (onsets) are reviewed each time you do a Reading/Writing Rhymes lesson. Once all of the rhyming words are written on a chart, students write rhymes using these words and read each other's rhymes. Because reading and writing are connected to every lesson, students learn how to use these patterns as they actually read and write.

For Reading/Writing Rhymes, make an onset deck using index cards. The deck should contain 50 beginning-letter cards:

- **Single consonants:** b, c, d, f, g, h, j, k, l, m, n, p, r, s, t, v, w, y, z

- **Digraphs:** ch, kn, ph, qu, sh, th, wh, wr

- **Blends:** bl, br, cl, cr, dr, fl, fr, gl, gr, pl, pr, sc, scr, sk, sl, sm, sn, sp, spr, st, str, sw, tr

Here's how to do a Reading/Writing Rhymes chart:

1. **At the beginning of the lesson, distribute all of the onset cards to students.** Depending on how many students are in your class, distribute **one, two, or three cards to each student.**

2. Once all of the onset cards are distributed, **write the spelling pattern you are working with 10–12 times on a piece of chart paper.** Write a line in front of each spelling pattern. As you write it each time, have students help spell it.

ack chart		
__ack	__ack	__ack
__ack	__ack	__ack
__ack	__ack	__ack
__ack	__ack	__ack

3. Then, invite each student who has a card that she thinks will make a word to place her card next to one of the written spelling patterns and pronounce the word.

- If the word is a real word, use the word in a sentence and write that word on the chart by adding the beginning letter(s) on the line in front of the spelling pattern.

- If the word is not a real word, explain why you cannot write it on the chart.

- If the word is a real word that does rhyme but has a different spelling pattern, such as **yak** to rhyme with **ack**, explain that it rhymes but has a different spelling pattern and include it at the bottom of the chart with an asterisk next to it.

- Begin names with capital letters, and if a word can be a name and not a name, such as **Jack** and **jack**, write it both ways.

4. When all students who think that they can make words with their beginning letters and the spelling pattern have added words to the chart, call students up to make the words that are not yet there by saying something like, "I think that the person with the **sl** card could add **sl** to **ack** to make a word we know."

- Try to include all of the words that any of your students would have in their listening vocabularies but avoid any obscure words.

- Add as many patterns to the chart as needed to write all of the words you can make.

5. Finally, if you can think of some good longer words that rhyme and have that spelling pattern, add them to the list. Spell and write each whole word on the chart under the other words because students do not have the letters to complete these words.

---

ack chart

back	Jack	crack
snack	jack	rack
tack	black	stack
track	pack	lack
quack	sack	shack
whack	slack	flack
hack	knack	smack
Mack	Zack	

backpack, fullback, haystack, ice pack

*yak, plaque

Once the chart of rhyming words is written, work together in a shared-writing format to write a couple of sentences using a lot of the rhyming words. After generating all of the **ack** rhyming words, one class came up with this silly rhyme:

Jack went back to the shack near the track to have a snack from his black backpack.

Next, students write rhymes. Many teachers let students work in pairs or teams to write these rhymes. Then, they read their rhymes to the class.

Alisha's and Ashley's Writing Sample

Mack, Jack, and Zack had a fun time running around the track. Mack and Jack told the duck to quack. Mack had a sack on his back. Zack stayed back. Zack ate a snack in an old black shack.

Ahmet's Writing Sample

Jack and Zack went out back to eat their snack but Zack stepped on a crack and broke his back. Jack took Zack to Dr. Mack and he said that Zack he broke his back. Zack sat in a chair but he sat on a thumb tack, it hurt so bad he ran out the front door and ran the track. He ran so fast he started to quack. He quacked so hard that he bumped into Jack. Jack had to go to Dr. Mack 'cause Zack headed for the tool shack.

Reading/Writing Rhymes Lessons

You can do Reading/Writing Rhymes lessons to teach any common spelling pattern. Below are some of the words students might use with the patterns **ad**, **at**, **en**, and **et**. For more Reading/Writing Rhymes lessons, see *Reading/Writing Simple Rhymes: Rhymes with One Spelling Pattern* by Patricia Cunningham and Dorothy Hall (Carson-Dellosa, 2003).

---

ad words

bad, Brad, Chad, clad, dad, fad, grad, had, lad, mad, pad, sad, tad, Tad, Thad

Conrad, Granddad, undergrad

*add, plaid

---

at words

at, bat, cat, fat, flat, gnat, hat, mat, pat, rat, sat, splat, that

acrobat, combat, doormat

---

en words

Ben, den, Glen, hen, Jen, Ken, men, pen, ten, then, when

Ellen, playpen, Steven

*been

---

et words

bet, Chet, get, jet, let, met, net, pet, set, vet, wet, yet

forget, Janet, sunset, upset

*debt, sweat

How Reading/Writing Rhymes Is Multilevel

Reading/Writing Rhymes is multilevel in much the same way that Making Words is multilevel. **The oral concept of rhyme and the idea that words that rhyme usually have the same spelling pattern are reviewed in each lesson. Beginning letters are also reviewed, and if students need a lot of practice with onsets, you can have them say the sound for each onset as you hand out the cards.** If some students still struggle with the simplest beginning sounds, give them the single-consonant cards and give the more-complex onset cards to your more-sophisticated readers. Adding some common words with different spelling patterns reminds students that when dealing with patterns, they have to think "usually," not "always." Also, as students write rhymes using the chart of words, they write on a variety of levels, but they all enjoy it. Be sure that you remind students to always spell the Word Wall words correctly. Students who have teachers that enforce this rule do this automatically. They know that **said** is not spelled like **Ted** because it is a Word Wall word and is spelled **s-a-i-d**.

Applying Strategies When Reading and Writing

Remember to make sure that your students are reading books on their own levels during Self-Selected Reading time. All students in second grade will be "really" reading (reading all of the words) if the right books are available. If some students cannot find good books (whether chapter books or those written for emergent readers), it may mean that these students will have to go to the library in your school or bring a book from home. Students who still need easy, predictable books also need a chance to read and reread these books at school. Speed, accuracy, and fluency come with practice. Students know when they are making progress, and some daily independent reading helps them develop these skills. It is also good for some students to reread stories or books you read as a class or with a small group at the beginning of the year. You and your students will be surprised when they see that what was once hard to read is now much easier. So, put those books and stories in your book baskets or on your library shelf for students to enjoy one more time.

At the end of the month, it is once again time to take stock of what those students who started the month behind their peers now know about words. In most second-grade classrooms, teachers have focused some attention on particular areas with these students during daily reading, writing, Word Wall, and other word activities. Even students who were struggling are making visible progress. Remember that you are assessing progress. Some students will take longer than others to develop these abilities, but if you see month-to-month growth based on your nudges during daily activities, you know that struggling students will eventually develop these critical understandings. For students who are making progress but are still not there yet, continue individual nudging for as long as necessary. **Our experiences with "won't give up" teachers tell us that second graders can eventually catch up if we do not give up!** The question is not *if* but *when*, and the answer depends on your willpower and determination to continue to assess and nudge.

December

Month at a Glance

December is always a busy month. Parents are busy, students are busy, and teachers are busy! Everyone is excited, and everyone has a lot to do. There are holidays to get ready for, and a vacation from school will cut this month short. It is hard to keep to a schedule, but students learn best when they have a routine.

Working with Words, along with the other three blocks, should continue. However, you should not introduce a new activity in December. A theme board is helpful for all of the words that your second-grade students want to use in their writing this month. This theme board can be filled with the special words used for the holidays and during December. It all depends on your students, your community, and what words students need for their self-selected writing. Use the excitement of what is going on to keep students interested in learning. This chapter includes some activities for December that you can get done along with all of the seasonal fun!

By the end of December, you will have **reviewed** the following:

- Word Wall words by writing new words that rhyme
- Use of holiday words on a theme board to write sentences
- Rounding Up the Rhymes with holiday books
- Guess the Covered Word lessons with holiday (and theme) words
- Making Words lessons with less cueing
- Reading/Writing Rhymes with high-frequency, short-vowel patterns
- Coaching during reading and writing

10 min.

Word Wall

Continue reviewing all of the words that are on the Word Wall and add a few new ones in December.

Theme Board

In addition to the Word Wall, **most teachers have theme boards that relate to the particular themes being studied.** In addition to pictures on the boards, the theme board contains words that help students write about the things they are learning. Imagine that you have a Happy Holidays theme board in your room and it contains the following pictures and words (and/or others appropriate for your students).

Holidays:	**December:**
Christmas	winter
Hanukkah	snow
Kwanzaa	vacation
New Year's Day	gifts
	presents
	Santa
	reindeer
	sleigh
	decorations
	dreidel
	candles
	menorah
	celebrate

Using Theme Boards

You can work on students' sentence-writing skills while having them practice Word Wall and theme words. On some days, dictate a sentence that is made up of words from your Word Wall and the theme board. Depending on what words you have on the theme board, you might include sentences such as the following:

This is **December**.	Others **celebrate Hanukkah**.
Christmas is coming.	People get ready for the **holidays**.
Some people **celebrate Kwanzaa** at this time.	Many homes have **decorations**.

Say each sentence while students listen and decide which word is on the theme board. Students see the word on the theme board (**visual**). Next, they cheer or chant the spelling of the word (**auditory**). Finally, they write the word (**kinesthetic**). Write the word with students so that they can self-correct the word and trace around its shape, following your lead. Students love to write about the holidays. Learning how to use words from the theme board and the Word Wall to write sentences helps move them along in their independent writing. It also helps students remember that holiday words are easy to spell if they just "read the room."

Rhyming Words

Imagine that you have five Word Wall words to review: **car**, **make**, **skate**, **truck**, and **clock**. After writing the words and self-correcting them, students are ready to turn over their papers. Ask students to do the following:

1. "On the top of the tree is a **star**." (Ask students which Word Wall word will help them spell **star**.) They decide that **car** will help and use the **ar** pattern to help them write **star**.

2. "Mom will **bake** cookies for the holidays." (Ask students which Word Wall word will help them spell **bake**.) They decide that **make** will help and use the **ake** pattern to help them write **bake**.

3. "Some children leave Santa a **plate** of cookies." (Ask students which Word Wall word will help them spell **plate**.) They decide that **skate** will help and use the **ate** pattern to help them write **plate**.

4. "I hope that Santa will not get **stuck** in a chimney." (Ask students which Word Wall word will help them spell **stuck**.) They decide that **truck** will help and use the **uck** pattern to help them write **stuck**.

5. "My **stocking** is red and very big." (Ask students which Word Wall word will help them spell **stocking**.) They decide that the word **clock** will help and use the **ock** pattern and the ending **ing** to help them write **stocking**.

Rounding Up the Rhymes

20–25 min.   There are many holiday books for December written in rhyme.

This Is the Dreidel by Abby Levine (Albert Whitman & Co., 2003)

First, read and enjoy this story with rhyming verse. Then, read it again and round up the rhymes. The fourth and last pages of this text are cumulative verse, and those rhyming words do not need to be written again. Write 10–12 rhyming pairs on index cards and put them in a pocket chart.

| shelf | choose | start | bright | another | frame |
| himself | use | heart | night | brother | name |

| door | plate | floor | about | Maccabee | declare |
| for | eight | anymore | out | free | there |

Next, have students underline the rhyming parts of the words.

| sh<u>elf</u> | ch<u>oose</u> | st<u>art</u> | br<u>ight</u> | an<u>other</u> | fr<u>ame</u> |
| hims<u>elf</u> | <u>use</u> | h<u>eart</u> | n<u>ight</u> | br<u>other</u> | n<u>ame</u> |

| d<u>oor</u> | pl<u>ate</u> | fl<u>oor</u> | ab<u>out</u> | Macc<u>abee</u> | decl<u>are</u> |
| f<u>or</u> | <u>eight</u> | any<u>more</u> | <u>out</u> | fr<u>ee</u> | th<u>ere</u> |

Then, discard the rhyming pairs that do not have the same spelling patterns.

shelf	bright	another	frame	about	Maccabee
himself	night	brother	name	out	free

Use these rhymes with the same spelling patterns to have students read and write some transfer words. Say, "What if you were reading and came to the word **light**. What words would help you write it?" Students decide that **bright** and **night** would help them write **light**, and they write it on their papers as you write it on an index card and place it under **bright** and **night** in the pocket chart. Continue with **smother**, **tame**, **shout**, and **three**.

shelf	bright	another	frame	about	Maccabee
himself	night	brother	name	out	free
	light	smother	tame	shout	three

Additional Rhyming Books

Other rhyming books you could use for Rounding Up the Rhymes in December include:

Angel Pig and the Hidden Christmas by Jan L. Waldron (Dutton Juvenile, 1997)

The Mouse Before Christmas by Michael Garland (Puffin Books, 2001)

The Night Before the Night Before Christmas by Natasha Wing (Grosset & Dunlap, 2002)

Guess the Covered Word

20–25 min. Continue to present Guess the Covered Word lessons. Let the holidays and celebrations keep your students involved. Using their names makes the sentences even better! You can also use sentences from the books and stories you have been reading to the class. Remember to include a variety of onsets.

December

My favorite holiday is **Hanukkah**.

The menorah is **bright** when it is lit.

Christmas is a holiday in December.

Some people celebrate **Kwanzaa**.

People get **presents** in December.

Holidays are **special** for families.

Keeping Warm

Karen wears a **sweater**.

Rocio wears his **jacket**.

A **sweatshirt** will keep you warm.

Kristen's **mittens** keep her warm.

Maurice's **shirt** is made of wool.

Everyone likes a **scarf** when it gets cold.

Holiday Gifts

Jeanne wants a new **sled**.

Tisha needs new **skates**.

Chrissie wants **skis**.

Mom's **gloves** need to be replaced.

Pilar wishes for **jewelry**.

Dad wants a new **shovel**.

Holiday Cookies

Grandma's cookies are the best.

She always lets **Stephanie** help her.

Joey's favorite cookies are **chocolate**.

Sometimes, Dahlia makes **cinnamon** cookies.

Mom likes **cocoa** with her cookies.

But, David likes **milk**.

20–25 min.

Making Words

If you started Making Words in August or September and did a number of easy lessons with five letters, including just one or two vowels, students were probably ready to move on to lessons with more letters, including two or three vowels, in October and November. **As you continue to make words, do less cueing than you did in early lessons.** For example, in early lessons, you say, "Change just the last letter . . . ." But, as you move along, you want students to think about what letters to change so you would be more likely to say, "Change just one letter . . . ." Here is an example of a good December lesson with seven letters, including two vowels, and less cueing:

candles
Letters: a e c d l n s

Step One: Making Words

"Take two letters and make the word **as**. Do it **as** quickly **as** possible."

"Change one letter in **as** to make the word **an**. I will get **an** ornament at the store."

"Now, add one letter and make **can**. You **can** do that."

"Make the three-letter word **and**. I will buy a gift for Dad **and** Mom."

"Add one letter to make **sand**. I put **sand** on my sidewalk when it is slippery outside."

"Change one letter in **sand** to make **land**. The **land** was covered with snow."

"Make one more four-letter word—**clan**. My **clan**, which is another word for family, will come to my house for the holidays."

"Add one letter to make **clean**. We will **clean** the house for the holidays."

"Start with new letters and make **dance**. I watched the people **dance** in *The Nutcracker*."

"Now, add just one more letter to turn **dance** into **dances**. Make the word **dances**."

"Make another six-letter word—**cleans**. She **cleans** the house before company comes."

"Now, use all of the letters to make the secret word." Give students one minute to figure out the secret word.

"Has anyone figured out the secret word?" Look around the room to see if anyone has the word in his holder. Have someone who has made **candles** come to the pocket chart and make it with the large letter cards. Then, have the other students check the words in their holders and say, "The secret word is **candles**. People light **candles** to celebrate the holiday season."

Step Two: Sorting Words

When students have made **candles**, draw their attention to all of the words that they made. These words are still in the pocket chart. Then, help students sort for a variety of patterns. Take the word **clan** and have students find the other words that begin with **cl**—**clean** and **cleans**.

Next, help students sort the words into rhymes.

an	and
can	sand
clan	land

Have students sort for related words. "Can you find two words that are related?" Lead students to find that **clean** and **cleans** are related. "Can you find two more?" Lead the class to see that **dance** and **dances** are related.

Step Three: Transferring Words

Remind students that rhyming words can help them read and spell other words. Write two words and have students use the sorted rhymes to decode them.

handstand   sandman

Say a few rhyming words and have students decide how they would spell them.

plan   grand   van   strand   grandstand

Here are a few other seasonal lessons that sort for beginning sounds and both long- and short-vowel patterns:

Making Words Lessons

Rudolph
Letters: o u d h l p r
Make: do, up, ho, hop, our, old, hold, hour, drop, uphold/holdup, Rudolph
Sort: h (ho, hop, hold, hour, holdup), -op (hop, drop), -old (old, hold, uphold), -our (our, hour)
Transfer: crop, shop, cold, scold, sour

holidays
Letters: a i o d h l s y
Make: as, is, his, has, had, hay, lay, old, hold, sold, lash, dash, daily, daisy, holidays
Sort: h (his, has, had, hay, hold, holidays), d (dash, daily, daisy), -ay (hay, lay), -ash (lash, dash), -old (old, hold, sold)
Transfer: pray, stay, cash, trash, gold

ornament

Letters: a e o m n n r t

Make: or, on, am, ram/arm, are, eat, neat, meat, mean, meant, ornament

Sort: m (meat, mean, meant), -am (am, ram), -eat (eat, neat, meat)

Transfer: jam, scram, seat, neat, heat

Christmas

Letters: a i c h m r s s t

Make: it, hit, sit, sat, hat, rat/art, mart, chat, cart, chart, start, Chris, smart, charts, Christmas

Sort: c (cart), ch (chat, chart, charts), chr (Chris, Christmas), -it (it, hit, sit), -at (sat, hat, rat, chat), -art (art, mart, cart, chart, smart), plurals (charts)

Transfer: knit, skit, slit, smart, dart

packages

Letters: a a e c g k p s

Make: as, sag/gas, peg, keg, age, ages/sage, sack, pack, page, cage, cages, pages, package, packages

Sort: s (sag, sage, sack), c (cage, cages), p (peg, pack, page, pages, package, packages), -eg (peg, keg), -age (age, sage, page, cage), -ack (sack, pack)

Transfer: beg, leg, stage, crack, track

Reading/Writing Rhymes

| 20–25 min. |

Work on short-vowel patterns this month with some Reading/Writing Rhymes lessons. One pattern that is fun to use during December is the **op** pattern. Write the pattern 10–12 times on a chart. Have students place the beginning letters in front of the rime to make words they know. Add as many patterns to the chart as needed to write all of the words that students can make. Remember to add words that rhyme but have different spelling patterns at the bottom of the chart with an asterisk.

op chart		
bop	flop	prop
chop	hop	shop
cop	mop	slop
crop	plop	stop
drop	pop	top

doorstop, gumdrop, hilltop, nonstop

*swap

....

Next, write a silly rhyme with the class, such as:

Let's st<u>op</u> and sh<u>op</u> for P<u>op</u>. Don't buy a m<u>op</u>. That will be a fl<u>op</u>!

Finally, let students write rhymes by themselves or in pairs. Then, have some students share their rhymes.

Reading/Writing Rhymes Lessons

Here are some rhyming words that students might use with the short-vowel patterns **ill**, **ot**, **ug**, and **ut** this month.

---

ill words

Bill, bill, chill, dill, drill, fill, frill, gill, grill, hill, ill, Jill, kill, mill, pill, sill, skill, spill, still, thrill, will, Will

anthill, fulfill, refill, uphill, windowsill

---

ot words

blot, clot, cot, dot, got, knot, lot, not, plot, pot, rot, shot, slot, spot, tot, trot

cannot, forgot, mascot, robot

---

ug words

bug, chug, drug, dug, hug, jug, lug, mug, plug, pug, rug, shrug, slug, smug, snug, thug, tug

earplug, ladybug, litterbug, unplug

*ugh

---

ut words

but, cut, glut, gut, hut, jut, nut, rut, shut, strut

coconut, haircut, shortcut, uncut

*putt, mutt, what

Here is a rhyme for the **ill** pattern:

B<u>ill</u> had his f<u>ill</u> of d<u>ill</u> and got <u>ill</u>. He took a p<u>ill</u> for the ch<u>ill</u>. Then, he sat on the windows<u>ill</u> and watched his dad gr<u>ill</u> with sk<u>ill</u>.

Applying Strategies When Reading and Writing

Coaching during Reading

The second way to help students use what they know is to conduct individual or small-group conferences when they are reading. When a student stops at a word, do the following:

1. Say, "Put your finger on the word and say all of the letters." Good readers look at all of the letters in a word automatically; that is why they get the words right. Removing one letter would change most words!

2. Then, remind the student, "Keep a finger on the word and finish the sentence." This way, the student can easily track back, find the word, and think of what would make sense.

3. If the student still does not know the word, remind her to use any picture clues that might be on the page.

4. If the troublesome word can be decoded with one of the spelling patterns on the Word Wall, say, "Let's see if you can use **house** to help you read **blouse**."

Helping students see that they can use what they know to figure out words is important for some students. Other students, however, use known words to figure out unknown words with little or no coaching.

The year has come to an end—but not the school year. Be anxious to return after the holidays because you will see those late bloomers beginning to bloom!

Coaching during Writing

The first opportunity to help students one-on-one each day is during the Writing Block. In second grade, students write every day, but not every piece is taken to a final copy. Just as **every piece that a writer writes is not always edited and published**. There are many words that students write that they can't be expected to spell, and when you conference with them, acknowledge their attempts and write the words correctly. For other words, such as those on the Word Wall or those words with familiar spelling patterns, students should be using what they know to get the correct spellings. Mention these words during your conferences too. "This word is on the Word Wall. You should have written it correctly. Write it now. These words have spelling patterns that we learn when we do On-the-Back activities. If you use the word **ride**, you can figure out the word **slide**." Writing conferences are good times to help students use what they have learned to write a lot of other words.

The writing conference is not always an editing conference. If students still need help getting thoughts on paper, help them with that. If students are writing run-on sentences, help them with that. **During a writing conference, everyone gets what he needs.** It isn't always an editing conference, but sometimes, it could be!

January

Month at a Glance

Happy New Year! January begins a new year and brings some old activities with a new twist. People in many areas are experiencing short days and long nights. The weather is cold, and many days people stay inside. Reading and writing are good activities to fill those long winter nights. Share with your students the book you are reading now (if you can) and the books you loved when you were young. Teach students more about winter—especially if it doesn't snow in your area—by reading informational books on what animals and people do in the winter. Students can also learn from good fiction books, like *The Snowy Day* by Ezra Jack Keats (Viking Juvenile, 1962). Penguins, hibernation, snowstorms, skiing, and shoveling snow are all winter subjects that help students learn about the world. Winter is a cold but magical time—even without snow.

The first weeks of January are great for learning in school. When many teachers come back from the holidays, they notice that their students who were struggling are now reading grade-level materials. When did it happen? It is almost as if they were given this gift for the holidays—only it did not come in a package. Now is a wonderful time to continue on this literacy journey. Your work is paying off! Students are rested and ready to learn even more.

Get back to the daily Working with Words routine right from the start in January. Have a time set aside for Word Wall practice and an On-the-Back activity every day! The second activity of the Working with Words Block will be Making Words two or three days a week, and the other days, you will choose from Reading/Writing Rhymes, Rounding Up the Rhymes, and Guess the Covered Word. Different students profit from different activities, so try to make it your New Year's resolution to do all of these word activities in your second-grade classroom this year!

By the end of January, you will have **introduced** the following:

- Alphabetical order as an On-the-Back activity

- Rounding Up the Rhymes with dinosaurs

- Guess the Covered Word lessons with an emphasis on two-letter blends

- Making Words lessons with an emphasis on two-letter blends and changing around letters to make new words

- How to plan your own Making Words lesson

- Reading/Writing Rhymes with an emphasis on long-vowel patterns

- Assessing word strategies used in reading, writing, and spelling at the midpoint of second grade

Word Wall

10 min.

The Word Wall is growing. Most second-grade Word Walls have 60–70 high-frequency words by the end of January. If you were to watch a teacher do the daily Word Wall activity of calling out five words for students to locate, clap or cheer, and write, you might conclude that all students were learning the same thing—how to spell the words. But, your conclusion would be wrong! Word Wall is actually a multilevel activity because students are at different stages of their word learning. **Students who have already learned to read the words on the wall are learning to spell them!** Unless your classroom is quite different from most second-grade classrooms, not all of your students have learned to read all of the Word Wall words. Some students need a lot of practice to learn to read these important high-frequency words. **When you call out words for students to locate, clap or cheer, and write, some students are getting the added practice they require to be able to read these words anywhere they see them.** Once students have learned to read these words, which might take several weeks or even months of practice, the very same Word Wall activity through which they learned to read them becomes the vehicle for them to learn to spell them. Meanwhile, students know which words are on the wall and can locate the words they need to spell when writing. In most classrooms, the rule is this: "Spell words the best you can, but if a word is on the Word Wall, you have to spell it right!" **There are also a few students in every second grade who are such fast word learners that they learned to both read and spell the words during the previous week's reading of a selection in which these words occurred!** What are they learning from the daily Word Wall activity? These super word learners are one of the reasons that most teachers combine handwriting instruction with the writing of the Word Wall words. Even fast word learners in second grade need reminders and modeling of how to make the letters so that their writing can be easily read.

On-the-Back Activities

Rhyming Words

On-the-Back activities also help even the fastest word learners. Continue to show students how some of the Word Wall words can help them read and spell a lot of rhyming words.

"All of the Word Wall words help you spell when you are writing. In fact, we are putting up these words because you see them over and over again when you are reading, and you use them over and over again when you are writing. It would be impossible to read and write without knowing your Word Wall words. **Some of the Word Wall words are particularly helpful because they help you spell a lot of rhyming words.** Let's work on that. One of the Word Wall words you practiced today was **name**. I will tell you some sentences to write that have words that rhyme with **name**. Listen for the rhyming word in each sentence, and we will decide together how to spell that word.

"What if you were writing, 'Soccer is my favorite **game**'?"

"Yes, the word that rhymes with **name** in this sentence is **game**, and we know that words that rhyme usually have the same spelling pattern. Let's write the first letter we hear in **game**, **g**, and then the spelling pattern in **name**, **ame**, to spell the rhyming word **game**."

Continue the lesson with these sentences:

My mother put my new picture in a **frame**.

We cooked our hot dogs over the **flame**.

When our team lost, I felt that we were all to **blame**.

Some kids have the **same** friends.

Notice that with these words, another spelling pattern (**aim**) rhymes. That is precisely why you come up with the examples rather than ask students to give you rhyming words. You are trying to teach them that most words that rhyme have the same spelling pattern. If you ask them for words that rhyme with **game**, they are likely to volunteer **aim** and **claim**, and they won't understand why those words don't work. If they do ask about other words, you can tell them that some rhymes have other possible spellings. Tell them that when this happens, they just have to know which one looks right, but at this point, you are happy if they begin to realize that spelling is not letter by letter, but is related to patterns. A second grader who notices two or more spelling patterns for a rhyme is ahead of a student who is still sound spelling all of the words that are not on the Word Wall.

To avoid confusion, you offer the examples, students decide which word rhymes, and you all decide how to spell it. **This activity moves the fast word learners along in their abilities to decode and spell unknown words. It is also good phonemic awareness training for students who are still struggling with the oral concept of rhyme.**

Sample On-the-Back Lessons for Rhyming Words

> **about: pout, scout, shout, sprout,** and **trout**
>
> **bug: dug, mug, hug, jug,** and **shrug**
>
> **crash: dash, flash, rash, trash,** and **splash**
>
> **drink: blink, mink, stink, shrink,** and **think**
>
> **float: boat, coat, gloat, goat,** and **throat**
>
> **found: ground, hound, pound, sound,** and **around**
>
> **house: blouse, mouse, spouse, doghouse,** and **outhouse**
>
> **joke: broke, choke, spoke, stroke,** and **woke**

Alphabetical Order

For this On-the-Back activity, second graders can take the Word Wall words that they are practicing or reviewing and write them in alphabetical order on the backs of their papers.

Kyla	ABC order
1. about	1. about
2. found	2. found
3. write	3. jump
4. then	4. then
5. jump	5. write

Rounding Up the Rhymes

Saturday Night at the Dinosaur Stomp by Carol Diggory Shields (Candlewick, 2002)

This book describes dinosaurs getting ready for a Saturday night dance. These dinosaurs are just like people in how they think, feel, and even enjoy the volcano's fireworks. **For the first reading, enjoy the book. The second reading may be an echo reading in which you read a line and students echo the line after you read it.** Keep a good beat and students will not only follow, they will also enjoy it. The third reading of the book is an appropriate time to call students' attention to the rhyming words. **As you read each page again, encourage students to listen for the rhymes as you say them.** As students identify the rhyming words, write them on index cards and put them in a pocket chart.

"Word went out 'cross the prehistoric **slime**:

Hey, dinosaurs, it's rock 'n' roll **time**!

Slick back your scales and get ready to **romp**

On Saturday night at the Dinosaur **Stomp**!"

Students should be able to tell you that **slime** and **time** and **romp** and **stomp** are the rhyming words on the first two pages. Write those four words on index cards and put them in the pocket chart. Instead of writing the words on index cards, some teachers use the board or a transparency. **The important thing is that once students hear the rhymes, they can then see the rhyming words. Some of the rhyming words will have the same spelling patterns (*slime* and *time*) and some will not (*shore* and *floor*).** When you are finished writing 10–12 rhyming pairs, the pocket chart will look like this:

slime	romp	shore	nails	splash	eggs
time	stomp	floor	tails	bash	legs

Maiasaur	bunch	stared	three	Ultrasauras	back
four	punch	scared	tree	chorus	whack

Get students to notice which rhyming pairs have the same spelling patterns and which do not by underlining the patterns. Have students help you discard rhyming pairs that do not have the same spelling patterns.

When you finish, these pairs will remain:

slime	romp	nails	splash
time	stomp	tails	bash
bunch	stared	three	back
punch	scared	tree	whack

Finally, do a transfer step and remind students that thinking of rhyming words can help them when they are reading and writing. **This transfer step is an important part of the lesson because it enables students to use what they know about words when they come to unknown words in their reading and writing.**

Write the word **dime** on an index card. Then, show it to the class, but don't say it. "What if you were reading and came to this word? What words in the pocket chart would help you read this word? Yes, **slime** and **time** have the same spelling pattern and rhyme."

Model the separating of sounds so that students will understand what to do when they come to a word and they know the spelling pattern but not the word.

"Let's see . . . **d—ime**. The word is **dime**. The candy cane cost a **dime**."

You may want to continue this for a few more words (**hunch** and **bee**) to give students more practice transferring these words to reading and writing.

slime	romp	nails	splash
time	stomp	tails	bash
dime			
bunch	stared	three	back
punch	scared	tree	whack
hunch		bee	

Additional Rhyming Books

Look for books written in rhyme that can be used to further students' words knowledge. There are many of these types of books in libraries and at bookstores. Other dinosaur books to read and enjoy this month include:

How Do Dinosaurs Eat Their Food? by Jane Yolen (Blue Sky Press, 2005)

How Do Dinosaurs Get Well Soon? by Jane Yolen (Blue Sky Press, 2003)

How Do Dinosaurs Go to School? by Jane Yolen (Blue Sky Press, 2007)

How Do Dinosaurs Say Good Night? by Jane Yolen (Blue Sky Press, 2000)

Guess the Covered Word

20–25 min.

Guess the Covered Word lessons in which some of the covered words begin with a single letter and some begin with two or more letters are important in second grade. **Be sure to uncover all of the letters up to the first vowel.** If you have uncovered **s** and a student guesses the word **snow**, tell the student that that was good thinking for **s**. Then, have everyone say **snow** slowly and listen for the **s** and **n**. Say, "My rule is that I have to show you everything up to the vowel, so if the word were **snow**, I would have to show you not just **s** but **n** too."

Here are some Guess the Covered Word lessons appropriate for January. The best lessons are those that you make yourself to follow up whatever your class is learning. Many teachers keep these lessons on a chart and cover the target words with sticky notes so that they can be reused the next year.

Winter Weather

In winter, it is often **snowy**.

Delano watches the **weather** on TV.

Sarah wants to know when it will **change**.

When it **freezes**, it is sometimes hard to drive.

Some people always buy **groceries** before a storm.

Animals in Winter

The bears are **hibernating** in caves.

The birds have flown south in a **flock**.

Many animals live under the **ground**.

Others have eaten and are **sleeping**.

In winter, many animals **scavenge** for food.

Snowman

Kim will make the **snowballs**.

Rusty has a **scarf** for him.

Mary has a **strawberry** for his nose.

Luis has **branches** for his arms.

Betty's **sweater** makes him look real.

Martin Luther King Jr.

Martin Luther King Jr. was a great **speaker**.

He **fought** for civil rights.

He worked hard for **freedom** for all.

Alejandro has a **video** about Dr. King.

There are many **stories** about him.

Brittany says, "He was a great **leader**."

Sea Otters*

Sea otters **dive** for their food.

They hold **food** with their front paws.

They take food to the **surface** to eat.

They lie on their **backs** when they eat.

* *Sea Otters* by Avelyn Davidson (Shortland Publicactions, 1998)

Any book you read to the class can be used for a Guess the Covered Word lesson.

Making Words

In December, secret words tied in with seasonal activities. In addition to being a word that ties in with a theme, unit, or seasonal activity, **the letters in a secret word must include specific examples from which to sort**. Here are some January lessons in which words begin with two-letter blends or with one of the two letters. There are also many words that students will have to stretch out to hear the two sounds as they spell the words.

1. First, sort the words according to their beginning letters—everything up to the first vowel.

2. Then, say some other words that begin with the blend and some that begin with one of the other letters and have students decide with which letters the words begin.

3. Finally, sort for rhymes and give students a few words to read and spell that rhyme and have the same spelling patterns. This will help students transfer their word skills when they are actually reading and writing. For these transfer words, continue to use two- and three-letter blends when possible.

Making Words Lessons

These lessons offer students a chance to see that when letters are moved around, they can make new words. The slash between words means that the letters in the first word are just moved around to make the next word.

snowman
Letters: a o m n n s w
Make: am, an, man, Sam, saw/was, won/now/own, sown/snow, swan, swam, woman, snowman
Sort: sn (snow, snowman), sw (swan, swam), -am (am, Sam, swam), -an (an, man, woman, snowman), -own (own, sown)
Transfer: jam, scram, plan, grown

snowball
Letters: a o b l l n s w
Make: so, was/saw, own, bow, low, blow, slow, slaw, ball, balls, bowls/blows, snowball
Sort: sl (slow, slaw), bl (blow, blows), -o (so), -ow (bow, low, blow, snow, slow), -aw (saw, slaw)
Transfer: go, grow, straw

mountains
Letters: a i o u m n n t s
Make: at, sat, mat, man, tan, tin, ton/not, into, tuna, Stan, stain, mount, amount, mountain, mountains
Sort: st (Stan, stain), -at (at, sat, mat), -in (tin), -an (man, tan), -ount (mount, amount)
Transfer: flat, spin, grin, than, count

blizzards
Letters: a i b d l r s z z
Make: is, lid, lad, lab, bid, bad, sad, slab, drab/Brad, raid, braid, lizard, blizzard, blizzards
Sort: br (Brad, braid), -ad (lad, bad, sad, Brad), -ab (lab, slab, drab), -aid (raid, braid)
Transfer: glad, Chad, crab, grab, maid

penguins
Letters: e i u g n n p s
Make: us, is, in, pin, pig, peg, pen, pens, spin/pins, pine, spine, penguin, penguins
Sort: p (pin, pig, peg, pen, pens, pins, pine, penguin, penguins), sp (spin, spine), -in (in, pin, spin), -ine (pine, spine)
Transfer: twin, skin, vine, twine, dine

football
Letters: a o o b f l l t
Make: at, bat, fat, fall, ball, tall, boot, loot/tool, fool, flat, boat, float, football
Sort: fl (flat, float), -at (at, bat, fat, flat), -oot (boot, loot), -ool (tool, fool), -oat (boat, float)
Transfer: splat, shoot, scoot, throat, spool

cheering
Letters: e e i c g h n r
Make: in, he, hen, her, ice, nice, rice, rich, inch/chin, grin, cheer, nicer, enrich, cheering
Sort: ch (chin, cheer, cheering), gr (grin), -in (in, chin, grin), -ice (ice, nice, rice)
Transfer: twin, twice, slice, price

Planning Your Own Making Words Lessons

It is fun to plan your own Making Words lessons to fit with themes. Here are the steps for planning a lesson:

1. Pick a secret word that can be made with all of the letters. In choosing this word, consider books that students are reading, theme words, and words that tie into something you are doing at school. Also, think about the letter sounds and patterns you want to call attention to during the sorting and transferring steps.

2. Make a list of words that students can make from these letters.

3. From all of the words you could make, pick approximately 15 words that include the following:

   - Words that can be sorted for spelling patterns that you want to emphasize

   - Little words and big words so that the lesson is multilevel

   - Words that can be made by arranging the same letters in different ways (**stop/post**) to remind students that when spelling a word, the order of the letters is crucial

   - A name or two to remind students that names need capital letters

   - Words that most students have in their listening vocabularies

4. Write all of the words on index cards and order them from shortest to longest.

5. Sequence the index cards to emphasize letter patterns or to reflect how changing the positions of the letters or changing/adding just one letter results in a different word.

6. Write each transfer word on an index card.

7. Store the cards in an envelope. On the envelope, write the words in the order you will make them, the patterns you will sort for, and several transfer words.

20–25 min.

Reading/Writing Rhymes

Reading/Writing Rhymes is popular with second-grade students. Students love making up silly rhymes using as many words as they can from the list generated from the onset deck (the 50 beginning sounds) and the chosen rime, or spelling pattern. Last month's spelling patterns were familiar short-vowel spelling patterns. This month, work on **ay**, **ake**, **ail**, **ale**, **aid**, **ade**, **ed**, and **ead**. Students are thinking as they choose words: "Does that have the right spelling pattern? Is that a Word Wall word?" What you see are amazingly correct spellings from students who have learned to think about words and spelling patterns in a sophisticated way.

Here is a list of words you can use for the **ay** pattern. Remember that the * means that the word rhymes but does not have the same rime.

---

ay chart

bay	may	stay
bray	pay	stray
clay	play	sway
day	pray	tray
fray	Ray	way
gay	ray	
gray	say	
hay	slay	
Jay	spray	
Kay		
lay		

Friday, replay, Saturday

*hey, neigh, prey, sleigh, they, weigh

---

1. First, make an **ay** chart, writing **ay** at least 10 times.

2. Next, pass out the cards in the onset deck. (Most teachers make the decks on index cards and reuse them.)

3. Students hold cards with the beginning letters next to the rimes to make words, and then say the words.

4. Sometimes, you will have to tell students that their letters will make words—and give them definitions.

5. When students have letters that don't make words with the **ay** spelling pattern, they give their cards to you. You may have to explain that the beginning letters make a word that rhymes but the word is spelled with a different spelling pattern. Then, write that word beside an asterisk.

6. Now, it is time for the fun—writing a silly rhyme with students. Here is an example:

> K<u>ay</u> and J<u>ay</u> went out to pl<u>ay</u>.
>
> They went to the b<u>ay</u>.
>
> They did not st<u>ay</u> because the d<u>ay</u> was gr<u>ay</u>.

7. Finally, students write rhymes by themselves or with partners. Listen to the conversations between partners and see how much students profit from this cooperative work. Have three or four students read their rhymes and you will see how much your students think as they write.

Below are some other patterns, including the words you can make for Reading/Writing Rhymes this month. Many rhyming words can be spelled with **ail** and **ale**. The same is true for **aid** and **ade**. The fact that there are two common patterns is not a problem for students when reading. Students quickly learn that both **ail** and **ale** have the long /**a**/ sound. When spelling a word, however, there is no way for students to know which is the correct spelling unless they recognize it as a word they know after writing it. This is why we sometimes write a word, think, "That doesn't look right," and try writing it with the other pattern to see if that looks right. When you write rhymes that have two common spelling patterns, write both patterns on the same chart. Students tell you the words their beginning letters will make, and you write them with the correct patterns. In many cases, there are homophones, words that sound the same but are spelled differently and have different meanings. Write both of these words and talk about what each one means. You may also draw a small picture next to one of these words so that students can tell them apart.

---

ake words

bake, Blake, brake, cake, fake, flake, Jake, lake, make, quake, rake, sake, shake, snake stake, take, wake

cupcake, mistake, pancake, snowflake

*ache, break, steak

---

aid/ade words

aid, braid,	blade, fade, grade,
laid, maid,	jade, made, shade,
paid, raid	spade, trade, wade
afraid, mermaid	lemonade, parade

*aide, stayed, grayed, suede

---

ail/ale words

bail, fail, frail, Gail,	ale, bale, gale,
hail, jail, mail, nail,	male, pale, sale,
pail, quail, rail, sail,	scale, stale, tale,
snail, tail, trail, wail	whale
Abigail, detail	female, tattletale

*braille, veil

---

ed/ead words

bed, bled, bred, fed,	bread, dead, dread,
fled, led, red, shed,	head, lead, read,
shred, Ted, wed	spread, thread, tread
bobsled	forehead, gingerbread

*said

Here are three examples of a student's rhymes using **ail/ale**, **aid/ade**, and **ed/ead**:

Gail got mail about a whale. It was a pale male with a tail.

She will nail the mail to the rail and put the whale up for sale.

The maid with the braid got paid.

She was afraid she would fade if not in the shade.

Ted and Fred led Mr. Ned to the bed in the red shed. Ted bled while he was sledding on the shiny red sled that he found on the bed in the red shed. Fred got sick and had to go to the bed in the creepy shed. "I don't like it in this creepy old shed in the small little bed," Fred said. Ted and Mr. Ned were having fun riding on the sled. But Fred was still in bed.

For more Reading/Writing Rhymes lessons, see *Reading/Writing Complex Rhymes: Rhymes with More Than One Spelling Pattern* by Cunningham and Hall (Carson-Dellosa, 2003).

Applying Strategies When Reading and Writing
Assessing Progress

Good assessment is an ongoing activity. Teachers watch their students in a variety of reading and writing situations and notice what strategies they are using and what they need to move forward. Many teachers designate one-fifth of their students to observe each day of the week. On Monday, their clipboard contains the anecdotal record sheets for the Monday students. Teachers write down what they notice about the reading and writing strategies that these Monday students are using. At the end of Monday, they file away the Monday sheets and attach to their clipboards the record sheets for the Tuesday students. This procedure makes the notion of anecdotal records workable and ensures that no student gets lost in the shuffle because each student gets noticed on a weekly schedule.

These ongoing observations of students let teachers know what many students are ready to learn. They also remind teachers what types of nudges particular students need. In addition, it is good to assess progress in a more systematic way from time to time. For many teachers, the halfway point in second grade is a good time to do some more systematic assessment. You can assess these strategies by looking at students' actual reading and writing. **Remembering the principle "What they don't use, they don't have!", assess students' decoding and spelling as they are actually reading and writing.**

Observing Word Strategies in Reading

In observing students' reading, teachers can look at the errors or miscues that students make and then determine what word-identification strategies they are using. Good readers self-correct many of their miscues. This usually indicates that they are using context to check that what they are reading makes sense. **Successful self-correction is an excellent indicator that the reader is using all three cueing systems—meaning (semantic), sounding like language (syntactic), and letter-sound knowledge (graphophonic).** Some readers tend to overuse context; their miscues make sense but don't have most of the letter-sound relationships of the original word. Others overuse letter-sound knowledge. Their miscues look and sound a lot like the original words, but don't make any sense. By observing students' reading, you can determine what strategies they are using and what kind of instructional activities you might provide for them.

To look at students' word strategies while reading, you first must have something for them to read in which they make some errors—but not too many. **This instructional level is the level of a book or story in which the student correctly identifies at least 90–95% of the words and has adequate comprehension of what was read.** The text that the student reads should be something the student has not read before. Although the student may read more than 100 words, only the first 100 words are generally used for analysis.

Teachers use a variety of materials to do this assessment, depending on what is available and what the school system requires. Some teachers use passages in the assessment package that accompanies many basal reading series. Other teachers/schools have designated books as benchmark books. They use these books only for assessment purposes. They decide which book first graders could read at the 90–95% word-identification accuracy level early in the year and call this the preprimer level. Another book, which most first graders could read halfway through the year, represents the primer difficulty level. A third book is selected as end of first-grade level. **For second grade, they choose two books, one for early in the year and one for later in the year.** In schools where Reading Recovery® is used, some teachers use books designated by Reading Recovery® scoring to be at particular levels. Finally, some teachers use a published Informal Reading Inventory that contains graded passages from the preprimer level through eighth grade.

Regardless of what assessment materials you use, the procedure is the same.

1. Have the student read the text that you think will be at the instructional level. This text should be a text that the student has not read.

2. Tell the student that you cannot help her while she is reading. When she gets to a word that she doesn't know, she should do the best she can to figure it out.

3. Also, tell the student that she should think about what she is reading because after she has read, she will be asked to retell in her own words what the text is about.

As the student reads, record what she reads using procedures adapted from Marie Clay's (1993) system for taking a Running record. If you have made a copy of the text (or if you are using a passage from a basal assessment or an Informal Reading Inventory), mark right on the passage. If not, simply record on a sheet of paper. Here are the recordings for one student on one passage. To show that it can be done either way, the record is shown on a copy of the passage and on a Running record sheet. (Of course, you need to record it only one way!)

Where Do Storytellers Come From?*

Helen Cordero is the most famous artist of storytellers.

She was born in 1915 at the Cochiti Pueblo, in New Mexico.

She started making clay figures because making pots was too hard.

She remembered how children loved hearing her grandfather tell stories.

She made figures that looked like her grandfather. She covered them with little children.

She called these figures "Storytellers."

More and more people started to make storytellers.

Today, the word "storyteller" means any figure that is covered with children or baby animals.

Some artists made animals covered with baby animals.

Some artists made people covered with children.

Storytellers

Helen Cordero ✓ ✓ ✓ fam-us ✓ ✓ ✓

✓ ✓ ✓ ✓ ✓ ✓ ✓ Cochiti Pueblo ✓ New Mexico.

✓ ✓ ✓ ✓ (f) ✓ ✓ ✓ ✓ ✓

✓ sc ✓ ✓ ✓ ✓ ✓ ✓ sc

✓ ✓ (f) ✓ ✓ ✓ ✓ ✓ ✓ ✓ ✓ ✓

✓ ✓ ✓ (f) ✓

✓ ✓ ✓ ✓ ✓ ✓

✓ ✓ ✓ ✓ a (f) ✓ ✓ ✓ ✓ ✓ ✓ ✓

✓ ✓ ✓ ✓ ✓ ✓ ✓

✓ ✓ ✓ ✓ ✓ ✓

* *Storytellers* by Diana Yurkovic (Shortland Publications, 1998)

As you can tell from the sample, we use a simple marking system, and you should score only the first 100 words, even though the passage read might be somewhat longer.

- Put a check mark above each word that is read correctly.
- If the student misreads a word, such as **slick** for **slippery**, write the error above the word.
- If the student leaves out a word, circle that word.
- If the student self-corrects a word, write **SC** above it. **Self-corrected** words are counted as correct.
- If the student makes the same error more than once, count it only one time.

After the student has read the passage, have her close the book (or take away the passage). Ask the student to tell what the text is about. Ask questions needed to determine if she understood at least 70–80% of the information read.

In our example, the class was talking and reading about storytellers. Neither the teacher nor the class had read this book. The teacher told the class that this was about Helen Cordero from the Cochiti Pueblo in New Mexico. Students then began to read the passage. This student misread or left out four words, giving that student a word-identification accuracy rate of 96%. Comprehension was adequate. This passage appears to be at the instructional level for the student since the teacher did not count the names and places that she gave them. She did not help with any other words. We can now analyze the student's errors and self-corrections to determine what word strategies she is actually using. (If we wanted to determine the highest level at which this student could read, we would need to have her continue reading higher- and higher-level passages until word-identification accuracy dropped below the 90–95% level or comprehension fell below the 70–80% level.)

Looking at the words read correctly, errors, and self-corrections, we know the following:

- The student is developing a store of high-frequency words. Word Wall words are being read correctly (**was, because, children, made, them, little, more, people,** and **making**).

- The student is cross-checking meaning and letter sounds. The self-corrections were probably triggered by the meaning of the words in the sentence made after each initial error (**remembered, stories**).

- The student is using initial-letter knowledge. The words misread all began with the correct letters (**fam-us** for **famous, a** for **any**, and the student made the correct beginning sound each time she came to the word **figure** or **figures**).

- The student knows compound words (**grandfather, storyteller**).

- The student is unsure about what to do with some big words. The two words omitted were both polysyllabic words (**figure, figures**).

Since this passage was determined by this teacher to be about right for second grade, we can determine that at this level, the student is applying what she knows about sight words, meaning, and letter sounds while reading.

Imagine, however, that on this passage, the student being assessed had made only one error—giving her a word-identification accuracy rate of 99%—and had had adequate comprehension. We would, of course, be pleased because this passage is about right for most students in the middle of second-grade. The student being assessed is a better-than-average reader. But, what can we tell about that student's decoding? We might just decide that this student is moving along fine and that we don't need to know anymore. If we did feel the need to assess the student's decoding, however, we would need to find a passage for her in which her word-identification accuracy was in the 90–95% range so that we could see what strategies she uses for decoding unknown words.

On the other hand, imagine that a student makes 15 errors on this middle-of-second-grade passage. When a student is making that many errors, it is impossible to cross-check meaning and letter sounds because so much of the meaning is missing in all of the left-out or misread words. We can't make judgments about the student's decoding-while-reading abilities until we have the student reading a passage at the instructional level. We need to find a text in which the student's word-identification accuracy is at the 90–95% level with 70–80% comprehension. Then, we can analyze the errors on that passage.

Observing Word Strategies in Writing

Writing samples also show growth in word knowledge. Because writing results in a visible, external product, it is easier to determine what students are actually using. Look at two or three writing samples done by each student a month or more apart to determine progress in word development. **Look at students' spellings of high-frequency words and their attempts at spelling less-frequent words.** Here is a sample written by one second grader. Underlined words are on the Word Wall. Words in boxes are not on the Word Wall but are displayed on theme boards or in other

places in the room. Circled words are words that the student believes are not spelled correctly. The student spelled the remaining words as best as he could. What can you tell about the student's developing word knowledge by looking at this sample?

First, notice that all of the Word Wall words are spelled correctly. The fact that all of the boxed words are also spelled correctly shows that this student knows how to use the print in the room to help him spell words.

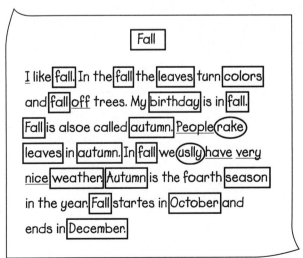

Next, look at how the student is spelling words that are not likely to be known by a second grader and are not readily available in the room. This student spelled **also** as **alsoe**, and **usually** as **uslly**. These are very good attempts at spelling and show that the student is able to hear sounds in words and knows what letters usually represent those sounds.

The next sample is taken from another second grader. Only a few words (underlined) are misspelled, and these incorrect spellings show a sophisticated understanding of letters, sounds, and spelling patterns.

> *C.J. and I*
>
> *C.J. and I are friends. We play together. We have fun. We like football. He wants to play on the Ttitns. He wants to be linebacker. I am Quarterback. He likes the Carolina Panthers and Wake Forest Demind Decins. We like to ride bikes.*

Finally, here is a writing sample from a student who is still struggling with words and spelling. The Word Wall words (underlined) are not spelled correctly in her first draft. Using the Word Wall would help this student. The only word seen in the room that was spelled correctly was her teacher's name. Although this student's word knowledge is not where you might expect the average second grader to be at this point in the year, almost all of the words are decipherable.

> *I lik Mrs. Boger*
>
> *She is vuere nise sum tims*
>
> *She is nise unuf to let us plae 7 up win it ranes*
>
> *the end*
>
> *I love you Mrs. Boger.*

In addition to writings on self-selected topics, many schools collect and look at focused-writing samples to determine growth in writing ability and word knowledge. **A focused-writing sample collected for assessment purposes should have a topic specified about which most students have good general knowledge. Students should write on this topic with no assistance from the teacher or any other student.** Some examples of topics used in primary classrooms include the following:

- My Friend
- Second Grade
- My Favorite Book
- My Favorite Author

Many schools have each student write about the same topic at several different points in time—May of kindergarten, January and May of first grade, and January and May of second grade, for example. These topic-focused, unassisted first drafts are then compared to determine an individual student's writing growth. In addition, a great deal of information is gathered about how the student writes—sentence sense, topic sense, word choice, writing conventions, etc. These samples yield valuable information about the student's developing word knowledge.

Sample #1   **George**

My Friends

Trey and Stephanie
Trey and Stephanie is my best friend. Sometimes thay play with me out side. Thay help Sometime with my eraly bird work. I love Trey and Stephanie. Thay love me to.

Sample #2   **Ashley**

My Friend

My friends name is Stephanie. She is a nice person. I like her. She is the best silly girl at school. She is kind to me. I like her very much! I sit bye Stephanie. She helped me on Thursday with the penguin picture. Her best friends name is Katy, Kristen, and Ashley. She is crazy. Now I sit with Stephanie. Every time I go to school I sit with her.

Sample #3   **Kelsy**

Katherine

I want to tell you about Katherine. Katherine is my best friend. She has brown hair and her eye color is hasal. Katherine has four pets, the are two dogs a cat, and a hamster. She goes to her dad's house on Friday. Her fairt food is fried okra and her favirt drink is grape colade. The animals she likes best are a chimack and a rabbit. Katherine is 7½ years old, and her birthday is Decmber 19th. Her favirt place to go is the mall. The best things Katherine likes about school are math and running the track. Katherine is a Browny Scout. Her best friend is Rachle. Rachle lives in Ohio. She has very nice illustashins. When Katherine grows up she want's to work at the bank. Her favirit show to watch is Figure it out, and her favirit book is Nobody's Mother is in Second Grade. She has one brother and she has two sister's. She lives in a two stoie house and has an atick and a basement. She has published two books at school. Her favirit restrant to eat at is Quinsy's. These are some thigs I know about Katherine.

Observing Word Strategies in Spelling Unknown Words

Finally, there is one more quick and simple measure to use halfway through second grade to determine how students are developing their word knowledge. Making sure that each student cannot see what others are writing, dictate 10 words that you don't expect them to be able to spell. Then, analyze their attempts. **Be sure to use a variety of words. The major criteria for the words are that they are not and have not been available in the room and that they show a variety of patterns.** Many teachers use the 10 words suggested by Gentry and Gillet on their Developmental Spelling Test (1992):

monster
united
dress
bottom
hiked
human
eagle
closed
bumped
type

(If your students like to write about monsters and have learned how to spell **monster**, you might substitute another word, such as **blister** or **mountain**.)

Once students have spelled these words as best as they can, Gentry and Gillet suggest analyzing their spelling using the following stages:

- **The Precommunicative Stage:** Spelling at this stage contains scribbles, circles, and lines with a few letters thrown in at random. Any connection between these letters and the words they are thinking is pure coincidence.

- **The Semiphonetic Stage:** The second stage can be seen when each word begins to be represented by a letter or two. The word **monster** may be written with **m**, **mr**, or **mtr**. Type might be written with **t** or **tp**. This stage indicates that the student is beginning to understand letter-sound relationships and knows the consonant letters that represent some sounds.

- **The Phonetic Stage:** In the third stage, vowels appear. They are not necessarily always the right vowels, but vowels are used and most sounds are represented by at least one letter. Phonetic spellings of **monster** might include **munstr** and **mostr**. **Type** will probably be spelled **tip**. You can usually tell when a student is in the phonetic stage because you can read most of what students in this stage write.

- **The Transitional Stage:** In this stage, all sounds are represented and each spelling is usually a possible spelling, just not necessarily the correct spelling. **Monster** in this stage might be spelled **monstir** or **monstur**. **Type** is probably spelled **tipe**.

- **The Conventional Stage:** Finally, the student reaches the stage of conventional spelling in which most words that a student at that grade level could be expected to spell correctly are spelled correctly.

Of course, **students' spellings of different words will indicate different stages.** Most second graders are beyond the Precommunicative and Semiphonemic Stages. You have been working to get them beyond the Phonetic Stage. The important thing is not which stage they are in but how they are growing. Put away the spelling samples, along with writing samples and running records, and use them to compare how students do on the same tasks toward the end of the year.

Students come to you at all different literacy and word levels, and they develop their literacy and word abilities at different rates. "Grade level" means "average." Students aren't now and never will be (and you shouldn't want them all to be) average! What you can expect and should document is growth. **Students come to you multilevel. Your instruction and assessment cannot deny this truth!**

February

Month at a Glance

February is here—that short but busy month. Winter is still with us; cold weather and storms are still expected in many places. Some schools have winter vacation so that families can enjoy the snow or escape and go to warmer climates. Some schools close when it snows, while other areas are so used to the snow that, unless there is a blizzard, they still have class! Still other parts of the country are warm, and students have heard of snow but have not seen it.

This month, there are many things to talk about in second grade at school—Valentine's Day, Dental Health Month, Washington's birthday, and Lincoln's birthday. In the United States, both birthdays are celebrated on Presidents' Day, but many teachers still celebrate each. This seems like a lot to do along with other themes that may be studied, such as animals in the winter. How can you get it all done in such a short month? Keep your routine of reading and writing about these topics with your class every day. Choose books to read that will help your students learn about the topics and model the writing of stories about the topics. Share what you know and how you learned about each topic. Use interesting words and activities to help students learn more about words.

By the end of February, you will have **reviewed** the following:

- An On-the-Back activity in which students drop **e**, double the consonant, or change **y** to **i** before adding the endings to words

- Rounding Up the Rhymes with holiday words

- Guess the Covered Word with a continued emphasis on two-letter blends

- Making Words with emphasis on two-letter blends, spelling patterns, and endings

- Reading/Writing Rhymes with more than one spelling pattern

You will have **introduced** the following:

- Reminders to use before and after reading and writing

- An On-the-Back activity in which students write sentences using Word Wall and theme words

Word Wall

10 min. Continue to add words to your Word Wall and make sure that your students are using them when they are writing, even in their first drafts. You want these words to be written correctly so that they won't be practiced wrong! You will probably have a February theme board that, in addition to pictures, contains words such as **Valentine's Day**, **valentines**, **cards**, **party**, **George Washington**, **Abraham Lincoln**, **president**, etc. Some of your second graders will want to add these words to their picture dictionaries. Continue to have students do On-the-Back activities to extend their word knowledge.

On-the-Back Activities

Writing Sentences

This On-the-Back activity will help students remember to use the theme board in addition to the Word Wall when writing. Say two simple sentences with Word Wall and theme words in each. Students write these sentences on the backs of their papers, using the Word Wall and theme board to help them. Here are some sentences you could use this month:

> I will **write** my **name** on my **valentines**.
>
> I have **cards** for my **friends**.

> Who was **George Washington**?
>
> He was the **first president** of the United States.

Adding Endings to Words

Another On-the-Back activity you might want to do this month is Adding Endings to Words. In this activity, students drop **e** before adding the ending to spell a Word Wall word. Imagine that the five Word Wall words you called out for students to locate, clap, or cheer, and write were these:

> make   phone   ride   skate   write

Have students turn over their papers, and say:

"Today, we will work on how to spell these Word Wall words when they need endings. I will say some sentences, and you should listen for the Word Wall word that has had an ending added."

I am **making** cookies after school.

I was **phoning** my friend when I lost the signal.

Tim was **riding** his new bike.

I like **skating** with my friends.

Hayden is good at **writing** stories.

After each sentence, students identify the Word Wall word and the ending. They decide how to spell it and write it on their papers. In this activity, students need to drop **e** before adding **ing**. Second graders need to learn and review this concept. On this day, focus on just this ending. On another day, you could also include some words that need to have **y** changed to **i** or a consonant doubled before the ending is added. This additional information about spelling words with a variety of endings and spelling changes really moves accelerated learners along in their writing abilities.

At least one day each week, make sure that all five words you call can have endings added to them. For Adding Endings to Words, read sentences that each contain one of the Word Wall words with the **s**, **ed**, **er**, or **ing** ending added. Students have to decide what the Word Wall word is and how to spell it with its ending.

Here are some words you might want to use to help students learn when to double the consonant:

stopping	stopped	joker	joked
phoned	having	tripping	tripped
skater	skated	writer	bugging
bugged	quitting	quitter	

Rounding Up the Rhymes

20–25 min.

There are many valentine books written in rhyme that you can use for February Rounding Up the Rhymes lessons.

The Night Before Valentine's Day by Natasha Wing (Grosset & Dunlap, 2001)

Students are getting ready for Valentine's Day by making beautiful valentine cards for their friends and classmates. Read this book to see what happens in one classroom when students are getting ready for Valentine's Day. Then, read the book again and round up the rhymes. Write the rhyming words on index cards and place them in a pocket chart.

| glue | read | mine | lace | name | beds |
| too | said | valentine | place | same | heads |

| day | white | bouquet | toys | faces | smiled |
| way | bright | away | boys | places | wild |

Next, have students underline the rhyming parts of the words:

| glue | read | mine | lace | name | beds |
| too | said | valentine | place | same | heads |

| day | white | bouquet | toys | faces | smiled |
| way | bright | away | boys | places | wild |

Then, discard the rhyming pairs that do not have the same spelling patterns. The chart now looks like this:

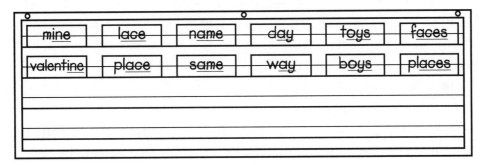

Finally, have students write some transfer words using these rhyming patterns. "What if it was writing time and you wanted to write, 'My friend was feeling **fine** even though she had a bad cold.' What words would help you spell **fine**?" Students decide that **mine** and **valentine** would help them write **fine**. Write **fine** on an index card and place it in the pocket chart under the words. Continue with **face**, **game**, **stay**, **joys**, and **traces**.

To show students what words helped you write the transfer words, your pocket chart will look like this:

Additional Rhyming Books

Other books you could read and use for Rounding Up the Rhymes in February include:

Jennifer Jones Won't Leave Me Alone by Frieda Wishinsky (HarperCollins Publishers, 1997)

Miss Spider's New Car by David Kirk (Scholastic, 1997)

Miss Spider's Tea Party by David Kirk (Scholastic, 1994)

The Night Before the Tooth Fairy by Natasha Wing (Grosset & Dunlap, 2003)

20–25 min.

Guess the Covered Word

The year is more than halfway over, and you might be tempted to stop doing Guess the Covered Word activities because many of your students know most of the beginning sounds in words. However, students don't really know something until they use it in their reading and writing. Guess the Covered Word focuses students' attention on all of the letters up to the first vowel—not just the first letter. In addition, Guess the Covered Word is the activity in which you teach and remind students that guessing based on only the first letters, how long the word is, or what makes sense won't help them figure out many words in their reading. **Guessing the word when they take all three cues—beginning letter(s) up to the first vowel, the length of the word, and what makes sense—will help students figure out the word more often than not.** In spite of all of the helpful On-the-Back rhyming activities and sorting and transferring during Making Words, there are students who never get very good at figuring out the vowel parts of words. **These students can become very good readers, however, if they can learn to cross-check beginning letters, length, and meaning.**

Continue with Guess the Covered Word lessons until the following occur:

- Almost all students represent almost all of the beginning letters correctly in their invented spellings.

- Students make guesses for unknown words during writing that begin with all of the right letters.

- Word guesses are about the right length.

- Word guesses make sense.

Activities like Guess the Covered Word help students do these things. Those students who have become good decoders and think automatically still enjoy the game because it does not take long and they are thinking and guessing with other students. All students like activities in which they are actively involved. Accelerated students probably come up with the accurate guess as soon as they see the beginning letter(s) because they have already used context to get close. They are able to use context, beginning sound, and word length. They are usually right with their guesses, and that is satisfying to them.

One day every week or two, write sentences, like the ones on the following page, on the board. Note that the word to be guessed is covered with two sticky notes and that the sticky notes are cut to reveal the length of the word. The first sticky note covers all of the letters up to the first vowel. Using themes, seasonal words, and students' names makes this activity more fun.

Remember that students' natural tendency seems to be to consider only the first letter. A student who guesses **subway** when the **sc** of **scooter** or the **sl** of **sled** has been revealed should be told: "That's a good guess for **s**, and it makes sense because you can ride on the **subway**. But, **subway** does not have **sc**. If it did, it wouldn't be a **subway**: it would be a **scubway**!" Some Guess the Covered Word activities for February are on the following page.

Valentine's Day

José gives **candy** on Valentine's Day.

Chocolate candy is Linda's favorite.

Some cupcakes have **hearts** on them.

Rolando gets **cards** from his friends.

John likes to write **poems** in his valentines.

When Winter Comes

Bears hibernate, and so do **snakes**.

Geese fly south for the winter.

Deer search for food in the **snow**.

Rabbits make **footprints** in the snow.

Michelle helps the animals by leaving **crumbs** outside.

Presidents' Day

Washington lived long ago.

He never told a **lie**.

Lincoln was honest too.

He had a **beard**.

We remember them on their **birthdays**.

Winter Fun

Carlos likes to ride on the **snowplow**.

Lamar rides on his **sled** down big hills.

Suzanne likes to **skate** in the winter.

Rusty likes to play his **trumpet**.

This winter, Molly learned to **ski**.

Making Words

20–25 min.

In most second-grade classes in February, single initial letters no longer need to be sorted for, since almost all students use these correctly to decode words while reading and to spell words while writing. If this is not true of your class, continue to sort first for beginning letters. **Always sort when you have two or more words that begin with two or more letters that have the same sound (such as *true* and *trust*).** Also sort for words with endings. When you have plurals or the same ending (**seeder** and **feeder**), put these together. If you just have two words like **feed** and **feeder**, talk about how they both have the word **feed** and that a **feeder** is the person or thing that **feeds** someone or something. Sort beginning letters and endings first, and end with the words sorted according to rhymes so that you can use the spelling patterns in these rhymes to read and spell some transfer words.

On the next page are some winter Making Words lessons that continue to focus on changing around letters to make new words, two-letter blends, and adding **s** to make a word plural. **Watch students to see if the two- and three-letter words are becoming automatic for those who were struggling at the beginning of the year.** See if students who had to say the word in order to spell it are now spelling words automatically. Students whose word knowledge is improving will use different strategies to spell the words. **Manipulating the letter cards helps some students see how words work.**

Making Words Lessons

animals

Letters: a a i l m n s

Make: is, as, am, an, man, aim, ail, mail, nail, sail, slam, slim, snail, salami, animal, animals

Sort: sl (slam, slim), -am (am, slam), -ail (ail, mail, nail, sail, snail), -an (an, man)

Transfer: scram, tram, trail, van, plan

hibernate

Letters: a e e i b h n r t

Make: be, bee, eat/ate, hen, Ben, been, beet, beat, heat/hate, Nate/neat, intern, hibernate

Sort: names (Ben, Nate), homophones (be—bee, beet—beat), -ee (bee), -eat (eat, beat, heat, neat), -en (hen, Ben), -ate (ate, hate, Nate, hibernate)

Transfer: free, cheat, treat, when, plate

raccoon

Letters: a o o c c n r

Make: on, or, an, ran, can, car/arc, oar, corn, acorn, cocoa, croon, raccoon

Sort: -an (an, ran, can) -oon (croon, raccoon), -orn (corn, acorn)

Transfer: bran, spoon, noon, horn, thorn

beavers

Letters: a e e b r s v

Make: be, bee, are/ear, bear/bare, save/vase, verb, bears, brave, erase, verse, serve, beaver, beavers

Sort: plurals (bears, beavers), -ave (save, brave), -ase (vase, erase)

Transfer: crave, slave, base, chase, chases

turtles

Letters: e u l r s t t

Make: us, use, let, rut, rust, rest, test, true, user, rule, rules, trust/strut, result, turtles

Sort: tr (true, trust), plurals (rules, ruts, turtles), -et (let), -ust (rust, trust), -ut (rut, strut)

Transfer: vet, yet, crust, shut, nut

feeders

Letters: e e e d f r s

Make: see, fee, fed, red, deer/reed, seed, feed, fees, free, freed, feeder, seeder, feeders

Sort: f (fee, fed, feed, fees, feeder, feeders), fr (free, freed), plurals (fees, feeders), -er (feeder, seeder), -ed (fed, red), -eed (seed, feed, freed), -ee (see, fee, free)

Transfer: three, free, bleeder, tweed, bleed

snakes

Letters: a e k n s s

Make: an, as, ask, Ken, sea, seas, asks, sank, sake, snake/sneak, snakes

Sort: s (sea, seas, sank, sake), sn (snake, sneak, snakes), plurals (seas, snakes), -ake (sake, snake)

Transfer: shake, flake, flakes, brakes, shakes

amazing

Letters: a a i g m n z

Make: in, an, am, aim, man, nag, zag, zing, gain, main, mania, again, amazing

Sort: -an (an, man), -ain (gain, main, again), -ag (nag, zag)

Transfer: clan, Spain, brain, brag, flag

Reading/Writing Rhymes

20–25 min.

Before beginning your Reading/Writing Rhymes lessons this month, ask students how they use what they learn in Reading/Writing Rhymes when they are reading and writing. Get them to explain that when they come to a word that they do not recognize immediately, they can often figure it out by thinking of a rhyming word that they do know. Explain that these rhyming words also help them with the last chunks of many longer words. **Get students to understand that good spellers spell by patterns and that rhyming words often have the same spelling patterns.**

Next, explain that many rhyming words can be spelled with two common patterns, as students saw last month and will continue to work with this month. How do students know which one to use? They need to have seen the words several times so that they know what looks right. For this month, you will work with four patterns: **ide/ied**, **eat/eet**, **ead/eed**, and **ite/ight**. When you make a chart, write both patterns. Words that do not fit either pattern but rhyme are written at the bottom beside an asterisk. Start with **ide** and **ied**.

First, make a chart:

ide/ied chart	
__ide	__ied
__ide	__ied
__ide	__ied
__ide	__ied
__ide	__ied
__ide	__ied
__ide	__ied
__ide	__ied

February

Then, pass out the onset deck of the 50 beginning-letter cards. Students come to the chart with the letters that they think make rhyming words. Then, they decide under which pattern to write each onset. Sometimes, the onset goes with both spelling patterns, like **pride** and **pried**. Explain this to students and give a sentence for each word.

Next, make up a silly rhyme with students:

The br<u>ide</u> will r<u>ide</u> ins<u>ide</u> to h<u>ide</u>.

The g<u>uide</u> stepped outs<u>ide</u> as she cr<u>ied</u> and l<u>ied</u>.

Finally, students make up rhymes by themselves or with partners. Some students write one line each, alternating lines with their partners, and these are some of the best rhymes!

Reading/Writing Rhymes Lessons

Here are other patterns to work with this month. Remember to use just one chart for two rhyming spelling patterns.

ide/ied chart	
bride	cried
chide	died
glide	fried
hide	lied
pride	pried
ride	shied
side	spied
slide	tried
stride	vied
tide	
wide	
beside	untied
inside	
outside	
*sighed	

eat/eet words	
beat	beet
bleat	feet
cheat	fleet
eat	greet
featheat	meet
meat	sheet
neat	sleet
pleat	street
seat	sweet
treat	tweet
wheat	
	parakeet
backseat	
mistreat	
repeat	
*Pete	

ead/eed words	
bead	bleed
knead	breed
lead	deed
plead	feed
read	freed
	greed
	heed
	need
	reed
	seed
	speed
	steed
	weed
mislead	agreed
proofread	indeed
*skied	

ite/ight words	
bite	blight
cite	bright
kite	fight
quite	flight
site	fright
spite	knight
sprite	light
white	might
write	night
	right
	sight
	slight
	tight
excite	daylight
	delight
*height	flashlight

Applying Strategies When Reading and Writing

In any classroom, the majority of time should be devoted to actual reading and writing. **The decoding and spelling strategies described in this book will be helpful to students only if they are reading and writing every day and beginning to employ these strategies as they read and write.** Here are some reminders that some teachers use for their students as they begin a reading or writing activity.

Before Reading:

"When we read, we come to words that we have heard but have never seen in print. When you come to an unfamiliar word, stop and say all of the letters in that word. Don't try to sound out each letter; just spell the word to yourself, naming all of the letters. If you can come up with a word, try it out and see if it makes sense. Remember that guessing a word based on just meaning, on just the first letters, or on just how long or short the word is, won't work very well. But, when you combine all three as we do in Guess the Covered Word lessons, you can make a good guess if the word is one that you have heard before."

After Reading:

Ask students for examples of words that they figured out either by saying all of the letters and looking in their word stores for words with similar patterns or by using meaning, all of the beginning letters, and word length. (Before reading, you may want to give students sticky notes and ask them to each write one word they figure out for themselves.)

Before Writing:

"As you are writing, concentrate on what you are trying to say—the meaning. When you finish writing but before you put away your piece for the day, reread it and look for any Word Wall words that you spelled incorrectly. Correct these spellings. Look for other words that you spelled as best as you could but that don't look right to you. Do you know rhyming words that might have the same spelling patterns? Write the words that way and see if they look right."

After Writing:

Ask students to give examples of Word Wall words that they fixed. Ask them to share examples of words that didn't look right and for which they tried different spelling patterns. Praise their efforts to monitor their spelling and apply what they are learning.

March

Month at a Glance

Whether March comes in like a lion or a lamb, spring will soon be here. March is magical with kites flying, leprechauns leaping, and pots of gold shimmering. Cold weather will soon be just a memory. Spring weather is greeted with enthusiasm. Light jackets and longer days are a welcome relief after winter. Students and their families have fun with kites, and as your students' kites soar, so do their spirits—they can read and they can write!

Students at this age have good attitudes if you let them know that they are making progress—and they should be! Green is the color of March, spring, and leprechauns. Don't let your little leprechauns trick you this month—they can read and write! Let them prove it to you as you become their cheerleader and celebrate their growing knowledge.

March is when many second graders become really good readers. If you have a few students who are still in need of extra nudges, this month's word activities might just be what they need. Have fun with words this month and continue to call on students who need a little more help to push them over the hump this month.

By the end of March, you will have **introduced** the following:

- On-the-Back activities that combine rhyming words and endings

- Rounding Up the Rhymes when rhyming words are not always at the ends of sentences

- Guess the Covered Word lessons that use paragraphs, not just sentences

- Making Words lessons that emphasize book/writing and holiday words, beginning-letter clusters, plurals, homophones, and changing around letters to make new words

- Reading/Writing Rhymes with **o** vowel patterns

- Using Words You Know as a strategy to read and write unknown, or less-familiar, one- and two-syllable words

Word Wall

10 min. Your Word Wall will probably have 100 words or more by the end of this month. The helpfulness of having this many high-frequency words instantly available to students should be obvious by the fluency with which they are writing. Remember that if you invest an extra two to three minutes in an On-the-Back activity, you can greatly increase the utility of the words displayed on your wall, achieve some additional handwriting practice, and not waste the backs of those half sheets of paper!

On-the-Back Activity

Adding Endings to Rhyming Words

Continue to practice writing Word Wall words with **s**, **ed**, and **ing**, and don't hesitate to use words that require spelling changes. As long as you tell students about the spelling change before they write each word, they can all spell it correctly. Some of your fast word learners will learn that they need to drop **e** when they add **ing** to **write**, **have**, **make**, **ride**, etc., and double **p** when they add **ing** to **stop** or **trip**.

When adding a new word, such as **snap**, to the wall, you have the perfect opportunity to remind students that some words can help them spell a lot of other words. **This month, combine rhymes and endings for some of your words.** After calling out five words and having students self-correct them, have students turn over their papers and listen for the word that rhymes with **snap** in each sentence. **Next, students write these words on the backs of their papers.** In March, you could use these sentences:

1. We will **clap** when the kite is in the air.
2. The **map** showed where the pot of gold was hidden.
3. The **trap** was set to catch a leprechaun.
4. The **strap** would hold him tight.
5. The kites **flap** in the breeze.

Use rhyming words to combine rhymes and endings.

ed endings	
clap	1. clapped
map	2. mapped
trap	3. trapped
strap	4. strapped
flap	5. flapped

s endings	
clap	1. claps
map	2. maps
trap	3. traps
strap	4. straps
flap	5. flaps

ing endings	
clap	1. clapping
map	2. mapping
trap	3. trapping
strap	4. strapping
flap	5. flapping

Rounding Up the Rhymes

Have fun with Rounding Up the Rhymes again this month. Call on students who need extra help to tell you the words that rhyme. Have them underline the spelling patterns in the rhyming pairs and tell you whether the patterns are the same. Let them tell you which rhyming pairs to keep and which to discard. See if they can write the transfer words. If they write them correctly, let them know that they have done a good job!

Loud Lips Lucy by Tolya L. Thompson (Savor Publishing House, 2001)

In this book, a loudmouthed little girl develops a bad case of laryngitis. As Lucy searches for her voice, she discovers that she missed a lot of things when she was talking and not listening! Read the book and enjoy this story. Then, reread it and round up the rhymes. Remember to have students listen carefully because the rhyming words are not always at the ends of the sentences. Sometimes, there are two rhyming words in one sentence. If you rounded up the rhymes using the whole book, the list of rhyming pairs would be too long. So, do half of the book and round up 10–12 pairs. Be sure to praise your students for finding all of the rhyming words, even if you have to help them a little.

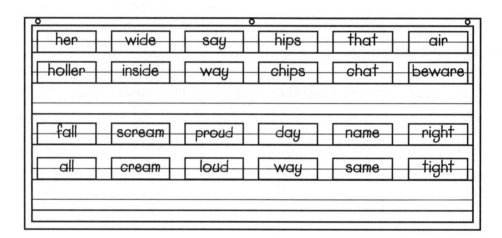

Next, have students underline the rhyming parts of the words:

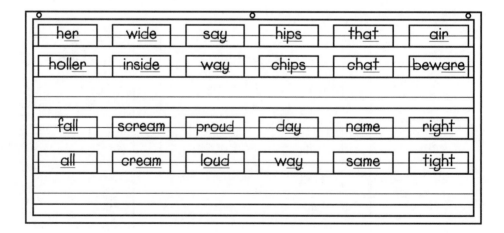

Then, discard the rhyming pairs that do not have the same spelling patterns:

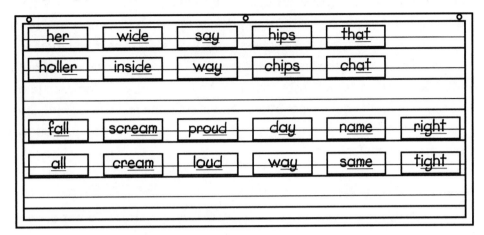

Finally, have students write some transfer words with these rhyming patterns. When they finish, their papers will have these words: **slide**, **trips**, **flat**, **hall**, **dream**, **tame**, and **bright**. Write the words on index cards and have students place them under the rhyming words that helped.

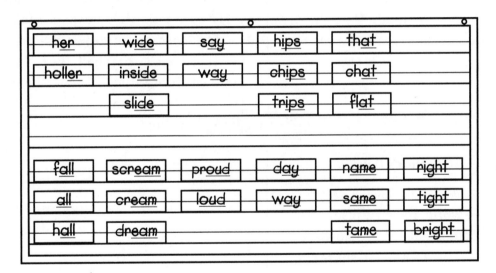

Additional Rhyming Books

Other books to use for Rounding Up the Rhymes in March include:

The Brand New Kid by Katie Couric (Doubleday, 2000)

It's St. Patrick's Day! by Rebecca Gomez (Cartwheel, 2004)

Today I Feel Silly and Other Moods That Make My Day by Jamie Lee Curtis (Joanna Cotler, 1998)

20–25 min.

Guess the Covered Word

Remember to provide cross-checking practice by giving students some sentences or a paragraph in which they have to guess some words—first with no letters showing and then with all of the letters up to the first vowel showing. This month, use paragraphs for Guess the Covered Word. Write each paragraph just as you did the sentences, covering each target word with two sticky notes—one for the beginning letter(s) and one for the rest of the word. Students should be getting good at using meaning, beginning letters, and word length to figure out words. Here are some examples appropriate for March:

March

Spring **begins** in March. It gets **windy** in March. Sometimes, I wear a **sweatshirt** to play outside. I can ride a **bicycle**. I can play with my **pet**. Some people fly kites high up in the **clouds**. The wind catches my kite and it **soars**. The wind blows my **clothes**. In March, I like to **stay** outside.

Here Comes Spring!

In March, spring begins. That means that nights get **shorter**. The weather gets warmer. Many students wear **jackets** to school. Other students wear **sweaters** in spring. The days are getting **longer**. Children can play outside after school. They can play **baseball**. They can ride their **scooters** up and down the street. It is fun to fly **kites** high in the sky. Spring is fun!

St. Patrick's Day

St. Patrick's Day is celebrated in March around the **world**. There are many **stories** about St. Patrick. One story says that he chased all of the **snakes** out of Ireland. This story is not true. The stories also talk about leprechauns and pots of gold. Leprechauns are **tiny**. They wear green **clothes** and shoes. To celebrate St. Patrick's Day, people wear **green**. Some big cities have **parades**. Sometimes, people who do not **wear** green on St. Patrick's Day get pinched!

Making Words

20–25 min. In addition to some March lessons using the words **Patrick** and **leprechaun**, do some lessons to focus on writing and illustrating words this month: **writers**, **author**, **artists**, **painter**, **pictures**, **notebook**, and **journal**. Continue to do some easier lessons as the year moves along. Some of your students are just beginning to get a sense of how words work, and figuring out the secret word occasionally is a great ego-booster. They are ready to understand that many words sound the same but have different spellings. Students have encountered these homophones on the Word Wall and in Reading/Writing Rhymes. These words can also be sorted for during Making Words, and several of the lessons for March are set up to do just that.

Making Words Lessons

journal
Letters: a o u j l n r
Make: or, on, an, Jan, ran, run, nor, jar, our, oar, loan, oral, lunar, journal
Sort: j (Jan, jar, journal), related words (ran—run), -or (or, nor), -an (an, Jan, ran)
Transfer: for, span, Stan, scan, plan

notebook
Letters: e o o o b k n t
Make: be, on, to, ton/not, knot, note, boot, book, took, nook, token, notebook
Sort: homophones (not—knot), compound words (notebook), -ot (not, knot), -ook (book, took, nook, notebook)
Transfer: jot, slot, plot, shook, brook

author
Letters: a o u h t r
Make: at, or, our, out, art/tar/rat, rot, hot, hat, hut, hurt, hour, auto, author
Sort: homophones (our—hour), -at (at, rat, hat), -ot (rot, hot)
Transfer: scat, splat, blot, spot, plot

artists
Letters: a i r s s t t
Make: at, sat, rat/art/tar, air, sit, sir, stir, star, tart, tarts, stars, stair, stairs, artist, artists
Sort: plurals (tarts, stars, stairs, artists), -at (at, sat, rat), -art (art, tart), -ar (star), -air (air, stair)
Transfer: splat, smart, jar, chairs, pairs

painter

Letters: a e i n p r t

Make: at, art/rat/tar, par, pat/tap, pen, pan, pant, part, rain, pain, paint, painter

Sort: -at (at, rat, pat), -ar (tar, par), -art (art, part), -ain (rain, pain)

Transfer: slat, splat, start, stain, scat

pictures

Letters: e i u c p r s t

Make: is, sip, sit, set, pet, pie, tie, ice, rice, price, purse, crisp, crust, cruise, picture, pictures

Sort: cr (crisp, crust, cruise), -et (set, pet), -ie (pie, tie), -ice (ice, rice, price)

Transfer: vet, lie, spice, twice, slice

writers

Letters: e i r r s t w

Make: we, wet, wit, sit, set, sew, tie, tire, wire, west, rest, tires, wires, write, writer, writers

Sort: plurals (tires, wires, writers), -et (wet, set), -it (wit, sit), -est (west, rest), -ire (tire, wire)

Transfer: yet, hire, fire, guest, guests

Patrick

Letters: a i c k p r t

Make: at, art/rat/tar, cap, tap, rap, part, cart, pack, tack, rack, pick, tick, trip, trap, trick, Patrick

Sort: t (tap, tack, tick), tr (trip, trap, trick), -ap (cap, tap, rap, trap), -ack (pack, tack, rack), -art (art, part, cart)

Transfer: slap, clap, stack, snack, chart

leprechaun

Letters: a e e u c h l n p r

Make: he, her, heel, heal, real, reel, each, chap, clap, clean, peach/cheap, lunch, preach, leprechaun

Sort: cl (clap, clean), ch (chap, cheap), homophones (heel—heal, reel—real), -ap (chap, clap), -eel (heel, reel), -eal (heal, real), -each (each, peach, preach)

Transfer: strap, feel, reach, beach, bleach

Reading/Writing Rhymes

20–25 min.

This month, work on some **o** vowel patterns. The **old/olled**, **ook**, and **oom** patterns are familiar to students and are used frequently when reading and writing. Write each pattern 10–12 times on a chart and pass out the onset cards. Here are some words you can make with the **old/olled** patterns:

old/olled words	
bold	polled
cold	rolled
fold	scrolled
gold	trolled
hold	
mold	controlled
old	enrolled
scold	
sold	
told	
retold	
unfold	
*bowled	

After completing the chart, write a silly rhyme with students.

One c<u>old</u>, b<u>old</u> day I s<u>old</u> my g<u>old</u>.

Don't sc<u>old</u>!

I was t<u>old</u> that my g<u>old</u> had m<u>old</u> and was <u>old</u>.

Finally, let students have fun writing their own rhymes. When they finish, have some students share their rhymes with the class. You will see that second graders are quite good at Reading/Writing Rhymes.

March

Reading/Writing Rhymes Lessons

Here are words you can write with the **ook** and **oom** patterns:

<table>
<tr><td>

ook words

book, brook, cook, crook, hook, look, nook, rook, shook, took

fishhook, mistook, notebook, unhook

*Brooke

</td><td>

oom words

boom, bloom, broom, doom, gloom, groom, loom, room, zoom

bathroom, bedroom, classroom, mushroom

*fume, plume, tomb

</td></tr>
</table>

The other patterns chosen for this month are **oke/oak** and **oat/ote.** Each of these rhymes can be represented by two spelling patterns. Sometimes, one of the patterns does not generate many words, such as **oak,** but you should still include it on the chart.

<table>
<tr><td colspan="2">

oke/oak words

</td><td colspan="2">

oat/ote words

</td></tr>
<tr><td>broke</td><td>croak</td><td>boat</td><td>note</td></tr>
<tr><td>choke</td><td>oak</td><td>bloat</td><td>quote</td></tr>
<tr><td>joke</td><td>soak</td><td>coat</td><td>tote</td></tr>
<tr><td>poke</td><td></td><td>float</td><td>vote</td></tr>
<tr><td>smoke</td><td></td><td>gloat</td><td>wrote</td></tr>
<tr><td>spoke</td><td></td><td>goat</td><td></td></tr>
<tr><td>stoke</td><td></td><td>moat</td><td></td></tr>
<tr><td>stroke</td><td></td><td>oat</td><td></td></tr>
<tr><td>woke</td><td></td><td>throat</td><td></td></tr>
<tr><td></td><td></td><td></td><td></td></tr>
<tr><td>awoke</td><td></td><td>afloat</td><td>devote</td></tr>
<tr><td>slowpoke</td><td></td><td></td><td>remote</td></tr>
<tr><td>*folk, yolk</td><td></td><td></td><td>rewrote</td></tr>
</table>

20–25 min.

Using Words You Know

Using Words You Know is an activity that helps students see that they can use what they know to figure out what they do not know. For example, second-grade students know the color words **red**, **green**, **brown**, and **black**.

1. Display the color words on the board or a chart and talk about the words.

2. Identify the spelling patterns **ed**, **een**, **own**, and **ack**.

3. Have each student make four columns on her paper, head the columns with the color words, and underline the spelling patterns.

4. Show students some **one-syllable words written on index cards**. Have them write these words under the words with the same patterns and use the rhymes to pronounce the words. **End with a two-syllable word so that students can see how to separate words and use this knowledge for bigger words.**

5. Say some one-syllable words and have students spell them by deciding with which words they rhyme. Then, say some two-syllable words. See if students can write them using both the spelling patterns in the last syllables and familiar words or word parts (prefixes).

Words to Read:

queen	knack	crown
shed	between	attack
touchdown	coed	

Words to Write:

smack	screen	sled
drown	backpack	unseen
fled	nightgown	downtown

Here is how a beginning chart looks:

red	green	brown	black
	queen		

Here is how a completed chart looks:

red	green	brown	black
shed	queen	crown	knack
coed	between	touchdown	attack
fled	screen	drown	smack
sled	unseen	nightgown	backpack
		downtown	

Applying Strategies When Reading and Writing

Many second-grade students are reading and writing well at this time of year. **You may want to look at some March writing samples from your struggling students and compare them to their January samples.** Is each student using the Word Wall and other words displayed in the room to correctly spell most words? Can you read the invented spellings of other words? Is there movement for most students from a letter-by-letter sound-match strategy to a spelling-pattern strategy? For example, the word **place** spelled **p-l-a-s-e** shows progression in word knowledge from the letter-by-letter spelling **p-l-a-s.**

You may also want to assess reading level and use of word strategies, particularly for those students whose reading levels were still at first-grade level or below in January. Can they now read more-difficult passages—with word accuracy of 90–95% and adequate comprehension—than they could two months ago? When reading at that instructional level, do their errors demonstrate use of context and/or beginning-letter sounds? Are they making some self-corrections? **Remember that all students will not read at the same level but that they should all be developing strategies and showing some growth in the difficulty of the text they can read.** Daily reading and writing will help all students improve. Look at what your students know to decide what you need to teach. Plan your mini-lessons for writing and word activities so that most students can learn something new and improve their word knowledge. Use individual conference time during the Writing and Self-Selected Reading Blocks to help students who need nudges and would profit from one-on-one instruction on their levels.

April

Month at a Glance

April is here, and spring has sprung! Vacation is on everyone's mind, including the teacher's. Most of us are in the final, and probably most difficult, quarter of the school year. Some students (and teachers!) have spring fever. The longer days bring soccer and baseball practice in the early evening. Parents are working in the yard at night or carpooling more often. Students have busier schedules, so finding time for reading and homework becomes a problem for some. Students have been working hard (like their teachers), and they are looking forward to a spring break. Other students are having such a good time with all of their friends and enjoying school activities that they would rather just stay in school, where they are successful and happy year-round! We have known both kinds of students and both kinds of teachers. We hope that everyone can enjoy a spring break and settle down for the last push. When students see themselves as successful readers and writers, they can and will continue to grow and learn. For these students, the literacy journey is a true ride, and spring won't stop them!

By the end of April, you will have **introduced** the following:

- Be a Mind Reader and other strategies for reviewing Word Wall words
- Rounding Up the Rhymes in which all students find success
- Guess the Covered Word with paragraphs and short and long words
- Making Words lessons in which students lead the sorts
- Reading/Writing Rhymes with **ar**, **art**, **orn**, and **ear/eer** patterns
- Using Words You Know with animal names to decode and spell words

10 min.

Word Wall

Try to get the last new words on the wall around mid-April. That gives you six weeks to review these words and greatly increases the chance that students will still be able to read and/or spell these words when they return to school in the fall. Although the Word Wall is helpful to your fast learners, who need some daily practice with handwriting and who profit greatly from the On-the-Back transfer to writing activities, it is not these students who need the Word Wall most. **The Word Wall is most helpful to students for whom learning the "often not spelled the way they sound" words is a huge chore!** It is better to put up just over 100 words by mid-April and do a lot of practice until the end of the year than to keep adding words. Fast word learners have probably already learned any words that you might add, and you won't have enough time to practice new words with your students who struggle to learn them.

On-the-Back Activities

Be a Mind Reader

Of all the On-the-Back activities, this will likely become students' favorite. For Be a Mind Reader, pick one Word Wall word. Have students number their papers from 1 to 5 as always, but this time, students will try to guess the word you have chosen. Give five clues to the word and let students write a guess after each clue is given. If a new clue confirms a student's previous guess, he can write the same word on the line that matches the new clue number. As you progress to the fifth clue, the word that you have in mind should become more obvious. By the last clue, all students should have the word. But, who read your mind and got it on the fourth clue? The third? The second? Or, maybe even the first clue?

Here are some clues for a Be a Mind Reader activity. Assume that all of the second-grade words listed on page 19 are on the Word Wall. **Give the clues one at a time and allow each student time to write a guess on her paper.**

Be a Mind Reader 1

1. It is one of the words on the wall.

2. It has five letters.

3. It begins with **r**.

4. It has only one syllable.

5. It makes sense in this sentence: Yes, you are _____. (right)

"Now, everyone has **right** on the last line, but who was a mind reader? Raise your hand if you had **right** on line four." A lot of hands will raise. "Raise your hand if you had **right** on line three." A few hands will raise. "Raise your hand if you had **right** on line two." Usually, one hand will raise—if someone is lucky! "Raise your hand if you had **right** on line 1." Miraculously, given the odds, every once in a while someone guesses the one word from all of the Word Wall words. That student read your mind!

Be a Mind Reader 2

1. It is one of the words on the wall.

2. It has four letters.

3. It begins with **t**.

4. The second letter is **h**.

5. It makes sense in this sentence: Cooper is taller _____ Grant. (than)

Be a Mind Reader 3

1. It is one of the words on the wall.

2. It has four letters.

3. It begins with **w**.

4. It ends with **h**.

5. It makes sense in this sentence: She likes to play _____ Asia. (with)

Be a Mind Reader 4

1. It is one of the words on the wall.

2. It begins with **s**.

3. It ends with **l**.

4. It has one syllable.

5. It makes sense in this sentence: I like to go to _____. (school)

Be a Mind Reader 5

1. It is one of the words on the wall.

2. It is a contraction.

3. It ends with **t**.

4. It has four letters.

5. It means "will not." (won't)

Adding Endings to Rhyming Words

In addition to Be a Mind Reader, continue to practice spelling words with endings and use rhyming formats to spell a lot of words. After most students get good at this, they can learn how to do both things at once. Here is an easy rhyming format with endings added. Read each sentence in which students need to identify and write a word that rhymes with **down** and has an ending added.

> The princess was **crowned** in the play.
>
> Her **gowns** were gold and white.
>
> She lived in two **towns** in one year.
>
> The **clowns** made us laugh.
>
> One was **frowning** and acting silly.

You could also do this activity with a harder format, using five different words to review and add endings to. Pretend that your students have just practiced the words **float, joke, quit, trip,** and **write.** Here are some sentences that you could use to identify rhyming words with endings:

> Travis is not **joking**.
>
> Yau is **quitting** the baseball team.
>
> Anton got hurt when he **floated** into the wall of the pool.
>
> Rita will not go on any **trips** in April.
>
> Karen is **writing** in a journal.

When students are writing, they often need to spell a word that rhymes with one of the Word Wall words and has an ending added. Make sure that everyone spells each word aloud correctly before writing it, because this could be frustrating for many students.

Rhyming Words

There is another rhyming On-the-Back activity that is worth mentioning again this month. It is harder this time, but closer to what students actually have to do to use the Word Wall words to spell words they need while writing. **To do this rhyming format, make sure that all of the words you call out have some words that rhyme and share the same spelling patterns.** You might call out the words **make, thing, mail, went,** and **will.** Help students notice that all of these words are helpful words (perhaps starred or stickered words on your wall). Tell students that you will pretend that you are writing and that you need to spell a word that rhymes with one of these five words. Say some sentences you might be writing, emphasizing the words you need to spell. Let students decide which of the five helpful words they wrote on the fronts of their papers will help you spell each word.

Caleb got new **brakes** on his bike.

Tandi put new **string** on her kite.

Laura **spent** her money at the game.

Liann ran fast, and I took a **spill.**

The **trail** in the park was long.

Once you have begun to use this new rhyming format, alternate it with the easier one in which your sentences use rhymes for only one of the words. The harder format helps students who are ready to think of a rhyming word that can help them spell a lot of words. The easier format is most important for students who are still developing their sense of rhyme and how rhyme helps them spell.

Rounding Up the Rhymes

20–25 min.

Although Rounding Up the Rhymes is an easy task at this time of year, it is still fun for students to do every other week. This is an easy activity that lets all second graders find success, and don't we all like to do things that we do well?

My Little Sister Ate One Hare by Bill Grossman (Dragonfly Books, 1998)

This is a fun book for young students, because it is so gross and at this age, they like gross things! It is the story of a little sister who has no problems eating things, like one hare, two snakes, and three ants, but when she eats 10 peas, she throws up and makes quite a mess! Read the book and enjoy it. Then, read it a second time and round up the rhymes on each page. It is a cumulative tale, so round up just the new rhyming words on each page. Write the words on index cards and put them in a pocket chart.

hare	snakes	ants	shrews	bats	mice
there	sakes	underpants	shoes	hats	twice

polliwogs	worms	lizards	peas	guess
frogs	germs	gizzards	these	mess

Next, have students underline the rhyming parts of the words.

h<u>are</u>	sn<u>akes</u>	<u>ants</u>	shr<u>ews</u>	b<u>ats</u>	m<u>ice</u>
th<u>ere</u>	s<u>akes</u>	<u>underpants</u>	sh<u>oes</u>	h<u>ats</u>	tw<u>ice</u>
p<u>olliwogs</u>	w<u>orms</u>	l<u>izards</u>	p<u>eas</u>	g<u>uess</u>	
fr<u>ogs</u>	g<u>erms</u>	g<u>izzards</u>	th<u>ese</u>	m<u>ess</u>	

Then, discard the pairs that do not have the same spelling patterns. These remain:

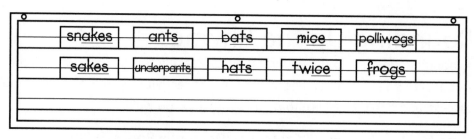

Finally, have students write some transfer words: **shakes**, **flakes**, **chants**, **flats**, **rats**, **dice**, and **jogs**. Write the words on index cards and put them in the pocket chart.

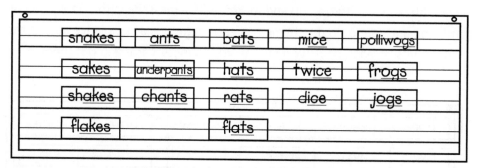

Additional Rhyming Books

Other books you could use for Rounding Up the Rhymes this month include:

Birds Build Nests by Yvonne Winer (Charlesbridge Publishing, 2002)

Butterflies Fly by Yvonne Winer (Charlesbridge Publishing, 2001)

The Night Before Easter by Natasha Wing (Grosset & Dunlap, 1999)

20–25 min.

Guess the Covered Word

Guess the Covered Word lessons provide practice with cross-checking by demonstrating to students that guesses based solely on meaning, beginning letters, or length are not good guesses. But, **when students combine all three to come up with a word that makes sense, has all of the beginning letters up to the first vowel, and is about the right length, they can make very good guesses at an unknown word.** Remember to have students make two or three guesses for each word with no letters showing. Then, uncover all of the letters up to the first vowel. If possible, cover some unusually short and long words so that students become sensitive to word length. Here are some example lessons that have some unusually short and long words:

April

In April, we can have fun at the **playground**. **Youngsters** swing and slide. Donna plays on the **bars**. Juan **runs** on the grass. Travis plays **basketball** with his friends. Our **classmates** come to watch us. They **yell** when we play well. What do you **do** in April?

Birds

Birds are many colors. Some birds build nests in **trees**. They use **twigs**, leaves, and grass. In their nests are **babies**. The baby birds **grow**. The mother bird brings the babies **food**. Soon, they learn to fly and **chirp**. We hear many birds **sing** as they sit in their nests.

Gardens

Every year, my **grandpa** plants a garden in his backyard. In the garden, he plants **tomatoes**, cucumbers, and radishes. Every time I visit, I get to **water** the garden. When the **vegetables** grow, I get to pick them. I like to eat **radishes** for a snack. First, I have to **wash** them. My grandpa lets me **sprinkle** a little salt on them. Food right from the garden tastes **so** good!

20–25 min.

Making Words

The most meaningful lessons are connected to what students are studying. You will notice that students who like Making Words will begin to guess the secret word the minute they see the letters. Continue lessons that are connected to the stories you are reading and the themes or units you are studying. You may want to continue to focus students' attention on blends. A lot of practice will help struggling readers see these beginning letters as clusters and look at all of the letters up to the first vowel. Remember that when you sort the words, you first sort for beginning letters, then for endings, and finally for rhymes. End with the rhyming words lined up under each other so that you can use them to read and spell a few new words. Also, remember to have students find the spelling patterns. Early in the year, you would get students to sort by saying:

"Who can find the two words that begin with **ch**?"

"Who can find the words with the **ing** ending?"

"Who can find all of the words with the **each** spelling pattern?"

Now, you say:

"Who can sort the words into words with the same beginning letters?"

"Who can find some words with the same ending?"

"Who can sort the words into rhymes with the same spelling pattern?"

Students need to look at words and see patterns. By this time of year, your questions should be leading them to that kind of independent thinking about the words they see.

Sometimes, let students decide what to sort for—they like this! They lead the class just as you have all year. If they do not choose a sort that you want to emphasize, you can add it at the end. Here are some April lessons for your class.

Making Words Lessons

detective
Letters: e e e i c d t t v
Make: it, tie, die, ice, dice, diet/tide/tied/edit, detect, device, deceive, detective
Sort: de (detect, device, deceive, detective), -ie (tie, die), -ice (ice, dice, device)
Transfer: pie, lie, spice, twice, price

project

Letters: e o c j p r t

Make: to, top/pot, pet, jet, jot, cot, crop, core, tore, rope, port, poet, crept, project

Sort: cr (crop, crept), -et (pet, jet), -ot (pot, jot, cot), -op (top, crop), -ore (core, tore)

Transfer: met, slot, flop, score, snore

playing

Letters: a i g l p n y

Make: in, an, pan/nap, pin, pig, pay, play, plan, pain, gain, plain, paying, playing

Sort: pl (play, plan, plain, playing), -ing (paying, playing), -an (an, pan, plan), -in (in, pin), -ay (pay, play), -ain (pain, gain, plain)

Transfer: spraying, scan, skin, spray, stain

glasses

Letters: a e g l s s s

Make: as, gas/sag, lag, sea, seas, seal/sale, legs, lass, glass, seals/sales, lasses, glasses

Sort: gl (glass, glasses), plurals (seas, legs, seals, sales, lasses, glasses), -ag (sag, lag), -ass (lass, glass)

Transfer: classes, grasses, brag, drag, class

crickets

Letters: e i c c k r t s

Make: it, kit, sit, tie, irk, ice, rice, tire/tier, kite, tick, trick, tricks, cricket, crickets

Sort: plurals (tricks, crickets), -it (it, kit, sit), -ice (ice, rice), -ick (tick, trick)

Transfer: clicks, chicks, split, twice, spice

cartoon

Letters: a o o c n r t

Make: cat, car, can, tan, tar/rat/art, cart, coat, torn, corn, acorn, actor, carton, cartoon

Sort: -an (can, tan), -art (art, cart), -orn (torn, corn, acorn)

Transfer: plan, scan, smart, thorn, scorn

waitress

Letters: a e i r s s t w

Make: at, sat, saw/was, wire, tire, wait, waits/waist, waste, water, write, waste, waiter, waitress

Sort: homophones (waist—waste), -at (at, sat), -ire (wire, tire)

Transfer: splat, scat, fire, inspire, hire

savings

Letters: a i g n s s v

Make: in, sin, sag/gas, nag, van, vans, vain, gain, sang, snag, sign/sing, assign, savings

Sort: plural (vans), -ag (sag, nag, snag), -ain (vain, gain)

Transfer: brains, chains, flag, shag, strain

Reading/Writing Rhymes

20–25 min.

Here are the steps to a Reading/Writing Rhymes lesson:

1. Distribute the onset cards to students. If students still need to practice with initial sounds, have each student say each onset as you pass out the cards.

2. Once all of the onset cards are distributed, write the spelling pattern with which you are working 10–12 times on a piece of chart paper.

3. Invite each student who has a card that she thinks makes a word to place her card next to one of the spelling patterns and pronounce the word. If the word is not a real word, explain why you cannot write it on the chart. If the word is a real word, use the word in a sentence and write it on the chart. If a word is a real word and rhymes but has a different spelling pattern, such as **planned** with **and**, explain that it rhymes but has a different pattern and include it at the bottom of the chart with an asterisk next to it. Write names with capital letters and if a word can be a name and not a name, such as **Bill** and **bill**, write it both ways.

4. When all students who think that they can spell words with their beginning letters and the spelling pattern have come to the chart, call students to make the words that are not yet there by saying, "I think that the person with the **tw** card could add **tw** to **ine** to make a word we know." If you use all of the patterns that you wrote to begin the chart, add as many patterns as needed.

5. If you can think of some good, longer words that rhyme and have that spelling pattern, add them to the list. Spell and write the longer words since students do not have the extra letters needed to make them.

6. Once the chart of rhyming words is completed, work together in a shared-writing format to write a couple of sentences using a lot of rhyming words.

7. Give students a few minutes to work individually or with friends to write some silly rhymes using as many rhyming words as they can.

For this month, use the spelling patterns **ar**, **art**, **orn**, and **ear/eer**. The **ear** and **eer** patterns are done on the same chart. Here are some words you can make with these patterns, along with the words that rhyme but do not have the same spelling patterns. (You may want to temporarily lose the **f** card when doing the **art** pattern!)

ar words	art words	orn words	ear/eer words	
bar, car, far, jar, mar, par, scar, spar, star, tar	art, Bart, cart, chart, dart, mart, part, smart, start, tart	born, corn, horn, morn, scorn, sworn, thorn, torn, worn	clear, dear, ear, fear, gear, hear, near, rear, smear, spear, tear, year	cheer, deer, jeer, leer, peer, sheer, steer, veer
ajar, boxcar, cigar, guitar	apart, depart, restart	acorn, foghorn, newborn, popcorn	appear	career, reindeer
*are	*heart	*mourn	*here, pier	

20–25 min.

Using Words You Know

Using Words You Know is an activity that helps students see that they can use what they know to figure out what they do not know. For example, second-grade students know the animal names **dog**, **cat**, **pig**, and **hen**.

1. Display these animal words on the board or a chart and talk about the words.

2. Identify the spelling patterns **og**, **at**, **ig**, and **en**.

3. Have each student make four columns on his paper, head the columns with the animal names, and underline the spelling patterns.

4. Show students some one-syllable words written on index cards. Have them write these words under the words with the same patterns and use the rhymes to pronounce the words. End with some two-syllable words so that students can see how to separate words and use this knowledge for bigger words.

5. Say some one-syllable words and have students spell them by deciding with which words they rhyme. Then, say some two-syllable words. See if students can write them using both the spelling patterns in the last syllables and familiar words or word parts (prefixes).

Words to Read:

sat	fog	fig
hog	pen	when
jog	gnat	flat
then	clog	chat
twig	smog	pigpen
nonfat	bullfrog	unclog

Words to Write:

bog	brat	wig
den	bulldog	splat
big	amen	combat
shindig	unpen	chitchat

The completed chart will look like this:

dog	cat	pig	hen
fog	sat	fig	pen
hog	gnat	twig	when
jog	flat	wig	then
clog	chat	big	pigpen
smog	nonfat	shindig	den
bullfrog	brat		amen
unclog	splat		unpen
bog	chitchat		
bulldog	combat		

Applying Strategies When Reading and Writing

If you are like most second-grade teachers, in April you probably have students who know a lot more about letters, sounds, and spelling patterns than they actually use when they are reading and writing. Who has made significant progress during second grade, and who is still struggling? Throughout this book, we have included reminders to students (and to you!) that the work you do with words is useful and worthwhile only if students actually use what they know while reading and writing. In On-the-Back activities, you create sentences like those that students would actually be writing and show students how Word Wall words can help them spell a lot of words. In Guess the Covered Word activities, you emphasize how to use meaning, all of the beginning letters, and word length to make very good guesses. By ending each Making Words and Rounding Up the Rhymes lesson with a few transfer words, you are constantly reminding students how and when to use their word strategies.

In spite of all of this concerted effort, there are still some students who just don't get it! They participate and seem to understand the word activities but when they read and write, they don't transfer what they know! There are two ways to help students use more of what they know.

Coaching during Writing

The first opportunity to help students use what they know occurs during writing conferences, when you are helping students fix their spellings in pieces that they will publish. In first grade, much of what students write stays in first-draft form, and their invented spellings are applauded. In second grade, focus on having students edit their own work—looking back to see if they spelled words correctly even in first drafts. Encourage a spelling consciousness by having students ask themselves when rereading their work, "Does it look right?" When you publish a book or prepare pieces for display on the bulletin board, help students spell the words correctly so that other people can read what they wrote. There are many words that students use in their writing that they can't be expected to know how to spell. When you are conferencing with students, simply acknowledge the good efforts shown in their invented spellings and write the correct spellings above them. But at other times, use the writing conference as the teachable moment to nudge students forward in their use of spelling patterns. Imagine that you are editing with a student at this time of year and the student has written **played** as **playd**. Ask that student:

> "What is the ending of that word? When we write Word Wall words with endings, what letters do we often add to words? Yes, that is right. One ending we add is **ed**. Now, check your ending and correct this word."

Writing conferences are a great opportunity to individualize what you teach students. For some students, just praise the invented-spelling efforts and fix the spellings. For other students, use the opportunity to point out things about letters, sounds, and spelling patterns that they know when they are doing word activities but are not applying as they are writing.

Coaching during Reading

To coach students to use what they know while reading, do some short (10–12 minutes) individual or very-small-group coaching sessions in which you lead students through the steps at the exact moments they need to use them. Use text that students haven't read and that contains some words they will need to figure out. Having text at instructional level (5–10 errors per 100 words) is ideal. Explain to students that the book will have words that they haven't learned yet and that the purpose of these lessons is to see how good readers figure out words that they don't know. Good readers are usually reading books they can read easily and fluently, stopping only once in a while to decode a word. Have a student begin reading, and when the student stops at a word, say:

"Put your finger on the word and say all of the letters."

Good readers look at all of the letters in each word. Students who are struggling with reading tend to look quickly at the word and if they don't instantly recognize it, they wait for someone to tell them the word. Asking students to say all of the letters forces them to look at all of the letters. **Sometimes after saying all of the letters, students correctly pronounce the word!** This is proof that they aren't in the habit of looking at all of the letters and you should let them know what they have done by saying:

"That's right. There are a lot of words that we see when we are reading that we don't recognize right away, but when we look at all of the letters, we can sometimes figure them out. Good job! Continue reading."

If, after saying the letters, the student does not say the word, you should say:

"Keep your finger on that word and finish the sentence."

It may seem foolish to have the student keep her finger there, but young students' print-tracking skills are not nearly as good as ours. Many students can't use the context of the sentence and the letters in the unknown word to figure out a word, because once they get to the end of the sentence, they can't quickly look back and find the troublesome word. **Keeping one finger on the word allows the student to quickly track back.** If, after finishing the sentence, the student correctly pronounces the word, say:

"Right. You can figure out a lot of words that you don't know if you use your finger to keep track of where the word is, finish the sentence, and do what we do in Guess the Covered Word—guess a word that makes sense, begins with all of the right letters, and is the right length. Continue reading."

If the student still does not get the word, you have three possible clues to point out. **If there is a good picture clue (that the student has ignored), you could say:**

"What animal do you see in the picture that begins with l?"

If the troublesome word can be decoded based on one of the patterns on the Word Wall or used frequently during other word activities, you could say:

"Let's see. The word is spelled **t-r-a-s-h.** We know that **c-r-a-s-h** spells **crash**. Can you make this word rhyme with **crash**?"

If there is nothing in the picture to help and the word is not easily decodable based on a familiar rhyming word, you can give an explicit context clue. Imagine that the word is **ridiculous** in this sentence:

That is a **ridiculous** hat.

Say to the student:

"Well, let's see. Do you think that it says 'That is a **ripe** hat' or 'That is a **ridiculous** hat'?"

The alternative word begins with the correct letter(s) but is so unmeaningful that the student will make the right choice. Then, say:

"Good. That was a hard word, but you got it! Let's continue reading."

Don't worry! Explaining this process in writing makes it sound much longer and more complicated than it actually is.

When you are coaching a student to learn to use what she knows (but isn't using), choose text in which the student will come to an unknown word every second or third sentence. When the student stops at a word, go through the following steps:

1. "Put your finger on the word and say all of the letters."

2. "Keep your finger there and finish the sentence."

3. "What do you see in the picture that starts with ——?"

   Or, "We see that the word is spelled——. We can spell ——. Can you make this word rhyme with ——?"

4. Finally, if all above cueing fails, say:
   "Let's see. Do you think that it says, '——' or '——'?"

When the student gets the word after any of your cueing, congratulate the student and point out which strategy he used to help him figure out the word.

If a student misreads a word (instead of the usual struggling-reader strategy of stopping on the word and waiting to be told), **wait for the student to finish the sentence, repeat the sentence as the student read it, and point out that it didn't make sense.** Then, take the student through as many steps as necessary.

Most students do not need the kind of one-on-one or very-small-group coaching described here, but for those who do, short coaching sessions held a few times each week, even at this time of year, make a world of difference in students' ability to use what they know when they need to use it!

May/June

Month at a Glance

The last month of the school year is finally here. All students and their teachers look forward to a break from the school routine. This is the time to continue sharing some good books and good authors with your students and to encourage reading as recreation. What better recreation is there on a hot day than to get lost in a good book under a shady tree? In just a few more weeks, students will leave second grade. Many students will be expected to have learned all about words and reading. They will now be expected to read to learn. Are they ready? You have been working hard all year, and this is a wonderful time to reap your rewards. You marvel at second-grade students who are reading and writing far beyond their years. You celebrate the gains made by your struggling readers—some have come so far this year! You realize that it is not where they are that matters but how far they have come. Often, growth in reading and writing is not steady but comes in spurts. When you see these spurts—and for some it happens in second grade—it is rewarding to both you and the student. You both have been working hard! During the last month, try to consolidate what you have been teaching and what students have learned this year.

By the end of the school year, you will have **reviewed** the following:

- Word Wall words and the many words students can write with rhyming words and endings
- On-the-Back activities that consolidate word learning with words on the wall
- Rounding Up the Rhymes to focus on vowel patterns and to have fun
- Guess the Covered Word with paragraphs and two-letter blends at the beginnings of the covered words
- Making Words with **y** and **z** and some summer words
- Reading/Writing Rhymes with the spelling patterns **oy** and **y /i/** using several charts to write some rhymes
- Using Words You Know with number words to read and write a lot of other words
- Consolidating many strategies taught and assessing the progress your students have made in their word learning

10 min.

Word Wall

This month, try to consolidate spelling the words on the wall, spelling words with endings, and seeing how some words help spell a lot of other words. Continue working with the important **s**, **ed**, and **ing** endings. Show students how they can spell **jumpy**, **rainy**, and **buggy** by adding **y** to **jump**, **rain**, and **bug**, and **nicely** and **friendly** by adding **ly** to **nice** and **friend**. You can add **er** and **est** to **new**, **little**, and **pretty**. **Tell, jump, kick, truck**, and **teach** can become the people who do those actions by adding **er**. Continue working with both rhyming formats and hope that all of your students will leave second grade with a firm concept that words that rhyme usually have the same spelling patterns and hope that many of your students will be spelling a lot of words based on other rhyming words.

You now have a good number of words on your wall that have opposites. Students enjoy Word Wall riddles, in which you call out each word by giving an opposite clue.

Word Wall Riddles

1. Word number one begins with **p** and is the opposite of **ugly**. (pretty)

2. Word number two begins with **g** and is the opposite of **boy**. (girl)

3. Word number three begins with **d** and is the opposite of **do**. (don't)

4. Word number four begins with **qu** and is the opposite of **start**. (quit)

5. Word number five begins with **r** and is the opposite of **wrong**. (right)

On-the-Back Activity

Be a Mind Reader

Perhaps students' favorite On-the-Back activity is Be a Mind Reader. In Be a Mind Reader, pick one Word Wall word and give five clues. Students number their papers from 1 to 5 as always, but they know that they are trying to guess the word that you are thinking of. As the clues progress, the word that you have in mind becomes more obvious. By the last clue, all students should have the word. But, who read your mind and got it on the fourth clue? The third? The second? Or, maybe even the first clue? Here are some Be a Mind Reader lessons. Assume that all of the words listed for second grade (page 19) are on the wall.

Be a Mind Reader 1

1. It is one of the words on the wall.

2. It has four letters.

3. It begins with **w**.

4. It ends with **t**.

5. It makes sense in this sentence: I _____ to the store. (went)

Be a Mind Reader 2

1. It is one of the words on the wall.

2. It has five letters.

3. It begins with **a**.

4. It ends with **out**.

5. It makes sense in this sentence: The story is _____ a fish swimming in the ocean. (about)

Be a Mind Reader 3

1. It is one of the words on the wall.

2. It has more than three letters.

3. It is a compound word.

4. It begins with a vowel.

5. It make sense in this sentence: The boy went _____ the water. (into)

Be a Mind Reader 4

1. It is one of the words on the wall.

2. It has five letters.

3. It is a homophone.

4. It begins with **th**.

5. It makes sense in this sentence: Put the shells over _____. (there)

20–25 min.

Rounding Up the Rhymes

The last month of school is a busy time with end-of-the-year activities, Mother's Day, Father's Day (if you go to school that late in June!), getting ready for summer, and talking about summer activities that students will take part in when they aren't at school. Remember the steps for Rounding Up the Rhymes:

1. Read the book and enjoy it!

2. Reread the book and have students round up the rhymes. You do not have to round up all of the rhyming pairs in the book; 10–12 pairs are enough.

3. Have students underline the rhyming parts of the words.

4. Discard any words that do not have the same spelling patterns.

5. Have students use the words that rhyme and have the same spelling patterns to read and write some transfer words.

Additional Rhyming Books

Here are some books that you could use for Rounding Up the Rhymes in May (Mother's Day) and June (Father's Day and summer vacation).

The Best Vacation Ever by Stuart J. Murphy (HarperCollins Publishers, 1997)

I Love You Because You're You by Liza Baker (Scholastic, 2006)

I Love You, Mom by Iris Hiskey Arno (Troll Communications, 1998)

Motherlove by Virginia Kroll (Dawn Publications, 1998)

My Daddy and I by P. K. Hallinan (Candy Cane Press, 2002)

The Night Before Summer Vacation by Natasha Wing (Grosset & Dunlap, 2002)

The 10 Best Things about My Dad by Christine Loomis (Cartwheel, 2004)

Guess the Covered Word

20–25 min.

It is time for students to consolidate the strategies of looking at all of the letters up to the first vowel, looking at how long the word is, and thinking what would make sense to decode an unknown word. **Try to get students to verbalize the strategies.** Ideally, they should all know that:

"When you see a word that you don't know, you can usually figure it out if you say 'blank,' finish the sentence, and guess a word that has all of the right beginning letters and makes sense in the sentence. It is good to look at how long the word is too."

Reinforce this by writing some paragraphs, such as the following, and cover each target word with two sticky notes. Read a paragraph, one sentence at a time, and have students make guesses for each covered word. As students continue reading, they should use the context of everything they have read to figure out the covered words. Be sure to have your sticky notes cut to size so that word length is obvious. When you remove the first sticky note, show students all of the letters up to the first vowel.

You don't always have to use the names of your students in Guess the Covered Word activities, as you have seen. But, using your students' names often keeps them actively involved, trying to figure out what happened to whom. You can also write some sentences that connect to your theme or unit. Remember to cover the words in various positions in the sentences. Be sure that students read each entire sentence, skipping over the covered word, before they give their guesses. Here are some paragraphs that use big words and two-letter blends at the beginnings of the words. **Notice that the words are placed in a variety of positions.**

May

We plant **flowers** in our garden. We plant **bright** flowers so that we can look at them all summer. We also plant **vegetables** in the garden. My favorites are tomatoes and **peppers**. We **water** our garden to keep it **growing**. **Harvesting** the vegetables is the best part. Do you have a garden?

Summer

In June, **summer** begins. The days get **long**. The sun is hot. When the weather is hot, people like to wear **shorts**. Sometimes, people go on **vacation**. Sometimes, they go to the **park**. Maybe I will go swimming in a **lake**. Often, the water is **cold**. People picnic in the summer. Some people pick **berries**. There are many interesting places to go and things to do in the summertime!

Second Grade

Second grade was **fun**. We learned how to **write** better. We became better **spellers**. In math, we learned **regrouping**. Everyone is getting **taller**. Some children have new **teeth**. Some have new **friends**. This summer, we will **relax**. Next year, we will be in third grade. I think that it will be **marvelous**!

20–25 min.

Making Words

There are many possibilities for Making Words lessons as the year draws to a close. You are reviewing many of the patterns and letter sounds that you have practiced all year, and for many students, they are becoming automatic. Some of the following lessons use the letters **y** and **z**. Do them in any order you choose and see how long it takes before students figure out the secret words! **Be sure to review that important names, like people's names and names of days of the week, begin with capital letters.** The days of the week make excellent lessons at any grade level. Many teachers like to have the **y** card be a different color from all of the other letters. It can't be the same color as the consonants or the vowels, because sometimes it is a consonant and sometimes it is a vowel! In addition to the usual things to sort for, lessons containing **y** words are sorted for the three sounds of **y**, as in **yam**, **fly**, and **family**.

Making Words Lessons

family
Letters: a f i l m y
Make: if, my, May/may/yam, Fay, fly, aim, ail, fail, mail, film, filmy, family
Sort: y (my, fly), y (filmy, family), -ay (May, may, Fay), -aim (aim), -ail (ail, fail, mail)
Transfer: stray, claim, exclaim, jail, snail

cooking
Letters: i o o c g k n
Make: in, ink/kin, coo, coon, cook, nook, nick, coin, oink, cooing, cooking
Sort: -ing (cooing, cooking), -in (in, kin), -ook (cook, nook)
Transfer: spin, spinning, brook, shook, looking

pretzels
Letters: e e l p r s t z
Make: pet, set, see, tree, step/pest, zest, reset, trees, steep, sleep, sleet, preset/pester, pretzel, pretzels
Sort: sl (sleep, sleet), st (step, steep), plurals (trees, pretzels), -et (pet, set, reset, preset), -ee (see, tree), -est (pest, zest), -eep (steep, sleep)
Transfer: yet, glee, chest, chests, sweep

diamond
Letters: a i o d d m n
Make: an, Dan, dad, did, add, aid, aim, mad, man, main, maid, mind, moan, nomad, diamond
Sort: -an (an, Dan, man), -ad (dad, mad, nomad), -aid (aid, maid)
Transfer: scan, glad, grad, paid, afraid

parents
Letters: a e n p r s t
Make: at, ant, art/rat/tar, pat, pet, set, sent, rent, rant, pant, past, paste, pants, parent, parents
Sort: plurals (pants, parents), -ant (ant, rant, pant), -at (at, rat, pat), -ent (sent, rent), -et (pet, set)
Transfer: plant, slant, spent, events, tents

scallops
Letters: a o c l l p s s
Make: all, cap, lap/pal, call, clap, slap, soap, pass, class, clasp/claps, scalp, scalps, scallop, scallops
Sort: plurals (claps, scalps, scallops), -ap (cap, lap, clap, slap), -ass (pass, class), -all (all, call)
Transfer: trap, traps, flaps, glass, stalls

summertime
Letters: e e i u m m r s t
Make: see, set, sir, sit, meet, must, rust, mist, stem, stir, tree, miser, steer/trees, time, summer, summertime
Sort: -ir (sir, stir), -ee (see, tree), -ust (must, rust)
Transfer: fir, free, spree, crust, trust

seashells
Letters: a e e h l l s s s
Make: he, she, see, sea, sell, seal/sale, heal, shell, leash, easel, easels, shells, leashes, seashell, seashells
Sort: plurals (easels, shells, leashes, seashells), -ell (sell, shell), -eal (seal, heal)
Transfer: spell, jell, squeal, squeals, meals

Reading/Writing Rhymes

20–25 min.

If your second-grade students are like most, they will enjoy Reading/Writing Rhymes lessons up to and including the last day of school. These lessons are fun for students to do in pairs or small groups. They keep students actively thinking and learning about words. Reading/Writing Rhymes also helps second-grade students learn the different vowel patterns, which makes them better readers and writers in the years to come.

Here are the steps to a Reading/Writing Rhymes lesson:

1. Distribute the onset cards to students. If students still need to practice initial sounds, have each student say each onset as you pass out the cards.

2. Once all of the onset cards are distributed, write the spelling pattern with which you are working 10–12 times on a piece of chart paper.

3. Invite each student who has a card that she thinks makes a word to place her card next to one

of the spelling patterns and pronounce the word. If the word is a real word, use the word in a sentence and write it on the chart. If a word is a real word and rhymes but has a different spelling pattern, such as **trail** with **whale**, explain that it rhymes but has a different pattern and include it at the bottom of the chart with an asterisk next to it. If the word is not a real word, explain why you cannot write it on the chart. Write names with capital letters, and if a word can be a name and not a name, such as **Jack** and **jack**, write it both ways.

4. When all students who think that they can spell words with their beginning letters and the spelling pattern have come to the chart, call students to make the words that are not there by saying, "I think that the person with the **br** card could add **br** to **ake** to make a word we know."

    If you use all of the patterns that you wrote to begin the chart, add as many patterns as needed.

5. If you can think of some good, longer words that rhyme and have that spelling pattern, add them to the list. Spell and write the longer words since students do not have the extra letters needed to make them.

6. Once the chart of rhyming words is completed, work together in a shared-writing format to write a couple of sentences using a lot of rhyming words.

7. Give students a few minutes to work individually or with friends to write some silly rhymes using as many rhyming words as they can.

For this month, use the spelling patterns **oy** and **y /i/**. Here are some words that you can make with these patterns, along with the words that rhyme but do not have the same spelling patterns (*).

oy words
boy, coy, joy, Joy, ploy, Roy, soy, toy, Troy
annoy, enjoy

y words
by, cry, dry, fly, fry, my, pry, shy, sky, sly, spry, spy, sty, try, why
apply, July, reply
* buy, bye, eye, hi, high, guy, tie, thigh

Let students write rhymes from two or more charts that you have already made.

Here is a rhyme using rhyming words from December that you can read with your class. Second-grade students are so good at writing rhymes that they are better than most teachers!

Bill and Jill had a spill going uphill. They saw a bug in their jug and gave a shrug. They could not stop. They had to shop. Off they went with a hop. They bought a pot and a cot, a drill and a grill. What a thrill for Bill and Jill!

To do a lesson with many rhymes, pull out charts from past months. Here are some rhyming words from December.

ill	op	ot	ug	ut
Bill	bop	blot	bug	but
bill	chop	cannot	chug	coconut
chill	cop	clot	drug	cut
dill	crop	cot	dug	gut
drill	doorstop	dot	earplug	haircut
fill	drop	forgot	hug	hut
frill	flop	got	jug	nut
gill	gumdrop	knot	ladybug	rut
grill	hilltop	lot	litterbug	shortcut
hill	hop	mascot	lug	shut
ill	mop	not	mug	strut
Jill	nonstop	plot	plug	uncut
kill	plop	pot	pug	*mutt
mill	pop	robot	rug	*putt
pill	prop	rot	shrug	*what
sill	shop	shot	slug	
skill	slop	slot	smug	
spill	stop	spot	snug	
still	top	tot	thug	
thrill	*swap	trot	tug	
will			unplug	
Will			*ugh	
anthill				
fulfill				
refill				
uphill				
windowsill				

20–25 min.

Using Words You Know

Using Words You Know is an activity that helps students see that they can use what they know to figure out what they do not know. For example, second-grade students know the number names **three**, **five**, **nine**, and **ten**.

1. Display these number words on the board or a chart and talk about the words.

2. Identify the spelling patterns **ee**, **ive**, **ine**, and **en**.

3. Have each student make four columns on his paper, head these columns with the number words, and underline the spelling patterns.

4. Show students some one-syllable words written on index cards. Have them write these words under the words with the same patterns and use the rhymes to pronounce the words. End with some two-syllable words so that students can see how to separate words and use this knowledge for bigger words.

5. Say some one-syllable words and have students spell them by deciding with which words they rhyme. Then, say some two-syllable words. See if students can write them using both the spelling patterns in the last syllables and familiar words or word parts (prefixes).

Words to Read:

bee	den	jive
mine	free	when
knee	dive	drive
then	amen	strive
pigpen	whine	airline
arrive	peewee	beehive

Words to Write:

men	pine	hive
live	flee	glee
twine	agree	playpen
spine	baseline	alive

This is how the completed chart will look:

thr<u>ee</u>	f<u>ive</u>	n<u>ine</u>	t<u>en</u>
bee	jive	mine	den
free	dive	whine	when
knee	drive	airline	then
peewee	strive	pine	amen
flee	arrive	twine	pigpen
glee	beehive	spine	men
agree	hive	baseline	playpen
	live		
	alive		

Applying Strategies When Reading and Writing

Don't give up! During editing conferences, remind students that every word needs a vowel and help them find and use the correct vowel patterns when writing words. Keep working with individuals or very small groups for short coaching sessions in which you remind students to use what they know when they need to use it. All students may not be perfect at doing this, but by the time school is out, they should all know that when they come to a word they don't know, they can:

1. Put a finger on the word and say all of the letters.

2. Keep the finger there and finish the sentence.

3. Look for something in the picture that starts with the letters, look at how the word is spelled to see if you know another word with that spelling pattern, or make sure that the guess makes sense and begins with the right letters.

Assessing Progress

Assessing progress at the end of the year means looking at how far students have come. Most teachers repeat whatever assessments they did halfway through the year. Many schools have assessment teams who go to each class and administer Informal Reading Inventories (IRI) to all students to determine their instructional reading levels. Information that will be helpful to next year's teachers is compiled in growth portfolios. In many schools, there are some items (focused-writing samples, IRI results, developmental spelling tests, etc.) that are included in all portfolios. Individual teachers—and sometimes students—then choose a few additional pieces to represent each student's growth. A short teacher write-up is usually included for each student. This short narrative describes the student's literacy early in the year and the growth that the student has made. Students come to you at all different stages of literacy development. Some students develop literacy, including decoding and spelling strategies, quickly and seemingly effortlessly. Other students take longer and need a lot of practice, nudging, and coaching. Assessment techniques should focus on progress and document growth. Such assessment allows you to do the kind of multilevel instruction that all students need and also allows you to celebrate how far each student has come, instead of bemoaning the fact that they are not all on grade level.

Overview

A Balanced Literacy Program

This chapter provides an overview of the entire Four-Blocks® Literacy Model of which the phonics and spelling activities described in this book are one component.

Each year, millions of students begin school in public schools in the United States. Some of these students can be immediately identified as "at risk"—the popular descriptor for those students who will not learn to read and write well enough to achieve a basic level of literacy and a high school diploma. The number of students at risk varies from community to community and state to state. In the United States, National Assessment of Educational Progress results suggest that more than one-third of all nine-year-olds cannot read at the basic level.

These statistics have held fairly constant despite decades of expensive attempts to fix the problem. Federal fix-ups have generally included a variety of pull-out remediation programs that have spawned huge bureaucracies and have not succeeded in eliminating the risk for very many students. State and local fix-ups have often consisted of passing regulations that prohibit students from being promoted unless they obtain certain test scores and have resulted in a huge number of students being retained. Shepard and Smith (1990) reviewed decades of research on retention. Their data show that retained students perform more poorly when they go to the next grade than they would if they had been promoted without repeating a grade and that almost any alternative is more effective than retention. Their data also suggest that "transition" classes, when they result in all students spending another year in the primary grades, have the same ill effects as retention.

Within individual schools or classrooms, in addition to federally provided remediation and state or locally mandated retention, teachers usually try to meet the needs of at-risk students by putting them in a bottom reading group and pacing their instruction more slowly. The data on bottom groups do not hold out much hope that this solution will ultimately solve the problem. Students who are placed in the bottom group in first grade generally remain there throughout their elementary school career and almost never learn to read and write up to grade-level standards (Allington, 1983; Allington, 1991).

Against this backdrop, we have the peculiarly American phenomenon of the "pendulum swing." Various approaches to reading come in and out of fashion. In 1990, when we began this endeavor, literature-based reading instruction (commonly referred to as "whole language") was the recommended approach. Today, this approach is not favored and school boards are mandating phonics approaches and purchasing spelling books. The search for the "best way to teach reading" denies the reality of individual differences. Students do not all learn in the same way, and consequently, approaches with particular emphases are likely to result in some students learning to read and others not. When the pendulum swings to another approach, we may pick up some of those who weren't faring too well under the previous emphasis but lose some who were. Forty years ago, the first-grade studies that were carried out to determine the best approach concluded that the teacher was more important than the method but that, in general, combination approaches worked better than any single approach (Bond and Dykstra, 1967).

This chapter describes the development of a framework for beginning-reading instruction that had two goals. The first goal was to avoid the pendulum swing and being trendy and rather, to find a way to combine the major approaches to reading instruction. The second goal was to meet the needs of students with a wide range of entering literacy levels without putting them in ability groups.

This project began in the fall of 1989 in one first-grade classroom (Cunningham, Hall, and Defee, 1991). This classroom was one of four first-grade classrooms in a large suburban school to which students from the inner city were bused. The class contained 26 students, half boys and half girls, 26% of whom were African American. The teacher was experienced and agreed to work with us to see if we could come up with a doable classroom framework for meeting the dual goals of (1) providing nonability grouped instruction that met the needs of students with a wide range of entering literacy levels and (2) providing students with daily instruction incorporating several reading approaches. During this first year, we developed the instructional framework and assessment procedures. At the end of this year, our success propelled us to involve other first-grade teachers at three schools. We refined the framework to accommodate the teaching styles of 16 unique first-grade teachers.

In the third year, we continued to work with first-grade teachers and students and expanded the program to second grade. From the fourth year on, we have worked with numerous school districts throughout the country to implement this balanced framework in hundreds of first-, second-, and third-grade classrooms.

As schools and school systems asked for a Four-Blocks® framework for their K–5 classrooms, we did not believe that a "one size fits all" approach would work, and added Building Blocks for kindergarten (*The Teacher's Guide to Building Blocks*™ by Dorothy P. Hall and Elaine Williams, Carson-Dellosa, 2000) and Big Blocks for the upper grades (*The Teacher's Guide to Big Blocks*™ by Amanda Arens, Karen Loman, Patricia Cunningham, and Dorothy Hall, Carson-Dellosa, 2005).

Finally, Pat Cunningham took a research leave from Wake Forest University to look at and work with schools across the United States that use the Four-Blocks® framework. Most of the children in the schools she visited were living in poverty and beat the odds—most were passing the state mandated tests. She reported on the results at the International Reading Association's Annual Conference in May 2006 and at the National Reading Conferences in 2005 and 2006. She also wrote about struggling readers in her *The Reading Teacher* column published in the December 2006/January 2007 issue.

The Instructional Framework

The instructional framework is the heart of the Four-Blocks program. The basic notions of this framework are quite simple, but its implementation is complex. There is much variation depending on how early or late in the year it is and in which grade the framework is being carried out. There is also much variation attributed to the teaching style of the teacher and the particular makeup of the class. In this section, we will describe the instruction and provide some sense of the variety that allows its implementation in a wide range of classrooms.

In order to meet the goal of providing students with a variety of avenues to becoming literate, instructional time is divided fairly evenly between the four major historical approaches to reading instruction. The $2\frac{1}{4}$–$2\frac{1}{2}$ hours allotted to language arts is divided among four blocks—Guided Reading, Self-Selected Reading, Writing, and Working with Words—each of which gets 30–40 minutes per day.

To meet our first goal of providing for a wide range of literacy levels without ability-grouping students, we make the instruction within each block as multilevel as possible. For each block, we will briefly describe some of the formats, materials, cooperative arrangements, etc., that we use to achieve this goal of multilevel instruction.

Guided Reading

In our first several years, we called this block the Basal Block because this was the time when the basal reader drove instruction. In recent years, teachers have branched out to use other materials in addition to or instead of the adopted basal reader.

Depending on the time of year, the needs of the class, and the personality of the teacher, Guided Reading lessons are carried out with the system-wide adopted basal; basal readers from previously adopted series; multiple copies of trade books or books from Wright, Rigby, or Troll; articles from *My Weekly Reader*; similar magazines and big books; or combinations of these. The purposes of this block are to expose students to a wide range of literature, to teach comprehension, and to teach students how to read materials that become increasingly harder. The block usually begins with a discussion led by the teacher to build or review any background knowledge necessary to read the selection. Comprehension strategies are also taught and practiced during this block. The reading is done in a variety of small-group, partner, and individual formats. Some teachers have a Three-Ring Circus or Book Clubs going on (Cunningham, Hall, and Sigmon, 1999). After the reading is completed, the whole class is called together to discuss the selection and practice strategies. This block sometimes includes writing in response to reading.

Early in second grade, most Guided Reading time is spent on grade-level books or the shared reading of predictable (easier) big books. Comprehension activities often include "doing the book," in which some students are given roles and become the characters as the rest of the class reads the book. Little books based on the big books are read and reread with partners, then individually or in small groups. Class books and take-home books patterned on the big book can be constructed in shared-writing activities. Often, the big books read during Guided Reading are chosen because they fit a theme or unit the class is studying, and they make Guided Reading time float seamlessly into other unit-oriented activities. Follow-up activities for the book and theme often occupy some of the afternoon time.

As the year goes on, the shared reading of big books continues to be a part of Guided Reading— often providing the easier-reading half of the grade-level and easier reading that we try to provide each week. Other books, not big and not predictable, are added. These books might be a part of a basal series, or they might be multiple copies of trade books. The emphasis shifts from reading together to reading with partners or alone. Instead of reading the selection first to students, as basals often suggest and teachers often do in first grade, second-grade teachers should let students read it first by themselves or with partners so that they can try to figure out new words. Teachers take students on a picture walk through the book, leading students to name the things in the pictures and to make predictions and pointing out a few critical vocabulary words with which students might encounter difficulty as they attempt the reading of the selection. Students then attempt the reading of the selection individually, with a partner, or in a small, flexible group with the teacher or another helper. The class reconvenes, discusses the selection, and sometimes reads it chorally or in some other whole-class format (not round-robin reading, however!). Comprehension strategies are taught and practiced. Predictions made before reading are checked. Story maps and webs are completed.

The next reading of the selection might include a writing activity. This writing activity is also done by some students individually, some with partners, and others in a group guided by an adult. This writing in response to reading is not a part of the Writing Block, however. Often, the next reading is an acting out of the selection, with various students playing different parts as the rest of the class reads or tells the story.

Making the Guided Reading Block Multilevel

Guided Reading is the hardest block to make multilevel. Any selection will be too hard for some students and too easy for others. We don't worry anymore about those students for whom grade-level Guided Reading material is too easy, because the other three blocks provide many beyond-grade-level opportunities. In addition, our end-of-year results always indicate that students who begin second grade with high literacy levels read well above grade level.

We do, however, worry about those students for whom grade-level selections are too hard. To make this block meet the needs of students who read below grade level, teachers make a variety of adaptations. Guided Reading time is not spent on grade-level material all week. Rather, teachers choose two selections—one grade-level and one easier—to read each week. Each selection is read several times, each time for a different purpose in a different format. Rereading enables students who could not read it fluently the first time to achieve fluent reading by the last reading. Students who need help are not left to read by themselves but are supported in a variety of ways. Most teachers use reading partners and teach students how to help their partners, rather than do all of their reading for them. While some students read the selection by themselves and others read with partners, teachers usually meet with small groups of students. These teacher-supported small groups change on a daily basis and do not include only the low readers.

In addition to the daily Guided Reading Block in which all students are included, many teachers schedule a 10-minute easy-reading support group in which very easy books are read and reread. This group of five to six students changes daily. All students are included at least one day each week. Students who need easy reading are included more often but not every day. One way or another, we try to ensure that every student has some Guided Reading instruction with instructional-level or easier material several days each week.

(For more information on Guided Reading, see Cunningham and Allington, 2006; and Cunningham, Hall, and Cunningham, 2000.)

Self-Selected Reading

Historically called individualized reading or personalized reading (Veatch, 1959), many teachers now label their Self-Selected Reading time Reader's Workshop (Routman, 1988). Regardless of what it is called, Self-Selected Reading is that part of a balanced literacy program when students get to choose what they want to read and to what parts of their reading they want to respond. Opportunities are provided for students to share and respond to what is read. Teachers hold individual conferences with students about their books.

In our classrooms, the Self-Selected Reading Block includes (and usually begins with) the teacher read-aloud. The teacher reads to students from a wide range of literature. Next, students read on their own level from a variety of books. In some classrooms, students read at their desks from crates of books that rotate from table to table. Each crate contains a wide range of levels and types of books, and students choose books from the crates. In other classrooms, students read at a variety of places. In addition to a reading center, many classrooms have a big-book center, a magazine center, a class-authored book center, a science center that includes informational books on the current science topic, a center full of books by a particular author being studied, a recorded-book listening center, and sometimes a computer center. At Self-Selected Reading time, students go to these centers. In some classrooms, they rotate through the centers on different days, and in other classrooms, they choose which center they want to go to.

Regardless of where students are, classrooms with successful Self-Selected Reading time all rigorously enforce the "No Wandering" rule. Once students get to their spots, they stay there!

A commonly observed phenomenon in homes in which four-year-olds have books and someone to read those books to them is what we call pretend reading. Young children want to do all of the things that the big people can do. They pretend to cook, to drive, and to be the mommy or the daddy, and they pretend that they can read. They do this pretend reading to a younger student or to a stuffed animal, and they do it with a book that they have insisted on having read to them over and over until they can "read" the book! (In fact, this insistence on having a favorite book read hundreds of times is probably motivated by their desire to learn how to read!)

Another way young children read books is by reading the pictures. This is usually done with an informational picture book on a topic of great interest to the student. The parent and the student have probably looked at "the airplane book" or "the dinosaur book" hundreds of times, spending more time talking about the pictures than actually reading the words. In fact, some of these books have wonderful pictures and sophisticated text, and parents don't read the text at all; they just lead the child to talk about the pictures.

We teach our early first graders that there are three ways to read. A few second-grade students need this information at the beginning of the year to be able to read independently. They can pretend read by telling the story of a familiar storybook. They can picture read by looking at a book about real things with a lot of pictures and talking about all of the things they see in the pictures. And, they can read by reading all of the words. Early in the year, we model all types of reading, look at books, and decide how students at their age would probably read each book.

> *The Gingerbread Man* is a book you could pretend read because you know the story so well. Let's practice how you might pretend read it if you chose it for Self-Selected Reading time."

> "How would you read this book about trucks? It has a lot of words in tiny print, but you could read it by picture reading. Let's practice picture reading."

> "Now, here is an alphabet book. You see just one word, and it goes with the picture. You can probably read this book by reading the words."

Once students know that there are three ways to read books, no student ever says, "I can't read yet!"

While students read, the teacher holds individual conferences with students. Most teachers designate students as Monday, Tuesday, Wednesday, etc., and conference with students on their days, spending three or four minutes with each student. Each student knows that on his day, he should bring one book that he has selected to share with the teacher. He reads (in whichever of the three ways is appropriate for that book) a few pages to the teacher and discusses the book and why he chose it. Thus, each student gets a short but dependable conference with the teacher each week to share what he likes about books.

(For more information on Self-Selected Reading, see Cunningham, Hall, and Gambrell, 2002.)

Making the Self-Selected Reading Block Multilevel

Self-Selected Reading is, by definition, multilevel. The component of Self-Selected Reading that makes it multilevel is the fact that students choose what they want to read. These choices, however, can be limited by what reading materials are available and how willing and able students are to read from the available resources. Fielding and Roller (1992) sum up the problem that many struggling readers have with Self-Selected Reading:

> "While most of the students are quiet, engaged, and reading during independent reading times, there are always a few students who are not. They are picking up spilled crayons, sweeping up shavings from the pencil sharpener, making trips to the water fountain, walking back and forth alongside bookcases, opening and closing books, and gazing at pictures." (p. 678)

The article goes on to indicate that many of the students who "wander round" during Self-Selected Reading time are the ones whose reading ability is limited and concludes the following:

> "Either they do not know how to find a book that they can read, or there is no book available that they can read or they do not want to read the books they can read. These students remind us of Groucho Marx: they refuse to become a member of any club that will accept them. In book terms, they cannot read the books they want to read and they do not want to read the books they can read." (p. 679)

Fielding and Roller make excellent and practical suggestions about how to support students in reading books they want to read, which would be too difficult without support, and how to make the reading of easy books both enjoyable and socially acceptable. These suggestions include helping students determine when a book is just right; encouraging students to read books that the teacher has read aloud; encouraging students to read with friends and to reread books they enjoy; modeling the enjoyment to be found in easier books; setting up programs in which students read to younger students and thus have a real purpose for reading engaging, easy books; and making a lot of informational picture books available. Although they do not use the term, following their suggestions would make the Self-Selected Reading time more multilevel. We have incorporated many of their ideas in the Self-Selected Reading Block, and in addition, we steer our more-advanced readers toward books that challenge them.

Writing

The Writing Block is carried out in Writer's Workshop fashion (Graves, 1994; Routman, 1988; Calkins, 1994). It begins with a 10-minute mini-lesson. The teacher sits at the overhead or with a large piece of chart paper. She writes and models all of the things that writers do (although not all on any one day). She thinks aloud—deciding what to write about and writes. While writing, she models looking at the Word Wall for a troublesome word that is there, as well as inventing the spellings of a few big words. She also makes a few mistakes relating to the items currently on the Editor's Checklist. When the piece is finished or during the following day's mini-lesson, students help the teacher edit the piece for the items on the checklist. Next, students do their own writing. They are at all different stages of the writing process—finishing a story, starting a new story, editing, illustrating, etc. While students write, the teacher conferences with individuals who are getting ready to publish. From three to five pieces, each student chooses one to make into a book. This piece is edited with the teacher's help, and the student proceeds to the publishing table where he will copy the edited piece and finally illustrate the book. This block ends with the Author's Chair in which several students each day share works in progress or their published books.

Early in second grade, the Writing Block begins with what we call the half-and-half stage. Students write on paper that is half lines and draw pictures on the other half. Drawing pictures helps some students visualize and, therefore, write better. For the mini-lesson, the teacher writes on a large sheet of chart paper or on a transparency. She thinks aloud and writes her sentences, telling students what she is doing and why. Sometimes, she does shared writing with students, letting them suggest sentences and tell her how to write them.

Next, students do their writing, and (if you have timed the move correctly) most students write a few sentences. The teacher goes around the classroom and encourages students. If asked to spell a word, she does not spell it, but rather she helps the student stretch out the word and write some letters. After 10–15 minutes, students make a circle and share their creations just as they did in the driting stage. The teacher responds positively to what they tell, including those few students who have only a picture! The next move is from the half-and-half stage to the stage in which students are writing on their own without teacher encouragement (stretching out words). The teacher can now spend the 15–20 minutes when students are writing to help students revise, edit, and publish pieces. This is also the time when we begin to use the Author's Chair procedure in which the Monday students share on Monday one piece they have written since last Monday, the Tuesday students share on Tuesday, etc.

For more information on the Writing Block, see *Writing the Four-Blocks® Way* by Cunningham, Cunningham, Hall, and Moore (Carson-Dellosa, 2005).

Making the Writing Block Multilevel

Writing is the most multilevel block because it is not limited by the availability or acceptability of appropriate books. If teachers allow students to choose their topics, accept whatever level of first-draft writing each student can accomplish, and allow them to work on their pieces for as many days as needed, all students can succeed in writing. One of the major tenets of process writing is that students should choose their topics. When students decide what they will write about, they write about something of particular interest to them and consequently something that they know about. Now, this may seem like belaboring the obvious, but it is a crucial component in making process writing multilevel. When everyone writes about the same topic, the different levels of students' knowledge and writing ability become painfully obvious.

In one of our classrooms, two boys followed each other in the Author's Chair. Jacob, a very advanced writer, read a book he had authored titled *Rocks*. His 16-page book contained illustrations and detailed descriptions of metamorphic, igneous, and sedimentary rocks. The next author was Nathan, one of the struggling readers and writers in the classroom. He proudly read his eight-page illustrated book titled *My New Bike*. Listening to the two boys read, the difference in their literacy levels was striking. Later, several students were individually asked what they liked about the two pieces and how they were different. Students replied that "Jacob wrote about rocks and Nathan wrote about his bike." Opinions about the pieces were divided, but most students seemed to prefer the bike piece to the rock piece—bikes being of greater interest than rocks to most children!

In addition to teacher acceptance, students choosing their topics, and teachers not expecting finished pieces each day, Writer's Workshops include two teaching opportunities that promote the multilevel nature of process writing—mini-lessons and publishing conferences. In mini-lessons, the teacher writes and students get to watch her thinking. In these daily short lessons, the teacher shows all aspects of the writing process. She models topic selection, planning, writing, revising, and editing, and she writes on a variety of topics in a variety of forms. Some days, she writes short pieces. Other days, she begins pieces that take several days to complete. When doing a longer piece, she models rereading what she wrote previously in order to pick up her train of thought and continue writing. The mini-lesson contributes to making process writing multilevel when the teacher includes all different facets of the writing process, writes on a variety of topics in a variety of forms, and intentionally writes some shorter, easier pieces and some more-involved, longer pieces.

Another opportunity for meeting the various needs and levels of students is the publishing conference. In some classrooms as students develop in their writing, students do some peer revising and editing and come to the teacher, the "editor-in-chief," for some final revising and editing before publishing. As teachers help students publish the pieces they have chosen, teachers have the opportunity to truly "individualize" their instruction. Looking at the writing of the student usually reveals both what the student needs to move forward and what the student is ready to understand. The editing conference provides the "teachable moment" in which both advanced and struggling writers can be nudged forward in their literacy development.

Finally, writing is multilevel because for some students, writing is their best avenue to becoming readers. Decades ago, Stauffer (1970) advocated language experience as an approach to teaching reading. Students found success because they could both read their own words (language) and comprehend their own experiences. When students who are struggling with reading write about their experiences and read it back (even if no one else can read it!), they are using their own language and experiences to become readers. Often, these students who struggle with even the simplest material during Guided Reading can read everything in their writing notebooks or folders. When students are writing, some students are really working on becoming better writers; others are engaging in the same activity, but for them, writing is how they figure out reading.

Working with Words

In the Working with Words Block, which is the focus of this book, students learn how to read and spell high-frequency words and learn the spelling patterns that allow them to decode and spell a lot of words. The first 10 minutes of this block are usually given to reviewing Word Wall words. The remaining 20–25 minutes are given to an activity that helps students learn to decode and spell words. A variety of activities are used on different days. Three of the most popular activities are: Guess the Covered Word, Making Words, and Rounding Up the Rhymes.

Making the Working with Words Block Multilevel

Throughout this book, we have described how the Working with Words activities are multilevel.

Connections across the Blocks

So far, we have been describing the blocks as separate entities. In most primary classrooms, each block has its allotted time, and you could tell which block the teacher and students were in if you watched. As much as possible, teachers try to make connections from one block to another. Many teachers take a theme approach. These teachers often select books for Guided Reading that correlate with their themes. During the writing mini-lesson when the teacher models writing, he often (but not every day) writes something connected to the theme. Some of the books teachers read aloud at the beginning of Self-Selected Reading and some of the books students can choose from are theme connected.

Theme words are not put on the Word Wall, which we reserve for high-frequency words and words that represent high-frequency patterns. But, most teachers have theme boards or charts in addition to the Word Wall. These boards change with each theme, and in addition to pictures, each board includes theme-related words that students will need as they pursue that theme. Often, the secret word in a Making Words lesson is theme connected. Sometimes, the sentences a teacher writes for a Guess the Covered Word lesson relate to the theme.

In addition to theme connections, there are other connections across the blocks. We practice Word Wall words during the Working with Words block, but we select them once they have been introduced in Guided Reading. We make sure that students know that when they are writing, they spell words as best as they can unless the word is on the Word Wall. Word Wall words must be spelled correctly!

Rounding Up the Rhymes occurs during the Working with Words block, but the book from which we round up the rhymes has usually been read by students during Guided Reading or read aloud by the teacher to begin the Self-Selected Reading Block. Sometimes, we do Guess the Covered Word activities by using sticky notes to cover one word on each page of a big book. We often introduce vocabulary during Guided Reading through picture walks, and while reading with small groups, we coach students on how to decode words using picture, context, and letter-sound clues.

In our mini-lesson at the beginning of each day's writing time, we model how we can find words we need on the Word Wall and how to stretch out words, listening for the sounds to spell big words not available in the room. When we help students edit, we praise them for their good attempts at spelling and coach them to use things they are learning during the Working with Words Block.

Most teachers who have organized their framework within the Four-Blocks® framework find that it is natural and easy to make connections across the blocks. By providing instruction in all four blocks, we provide students with many different ways to learn how to read and write. Connections across the blocks help students build bridges between what they are learning.

The Research Base for *Month-by-Month Phonics*

The *Month-by-Month Phonics* books for each grade level contain a variety of motivating, multilevel activities. These activities are also research-based. Research reviews (National Reading Panel, 2000; Stahl, Duffy-Hester, and Stahl, 1998) have suggested that the most effective phonics instruction is explicit, planned and sequential, and systematic. *Month-by-Month Phonics* meets all of these criteria.

Month-by-Month Phonics Is Explicit

It is generally agreed that phonics instruction can be explicit or implicit. Adams (1990) defines explicit phonics as "the provision of systematic instruction on the relation of letter-sounds to words" (p. 49). She defines implicit phonics as "the philosophy of letting students induce letter-sounds from whole words" (p. 49). *Month-by-Month Phonics* is not an "implicit phonics" program that expects students to "induce letter-sounds from whole words." At all levels of the program, students are explicitly taught letter-sound relationships and how these relationships transfer to decoding and spelling unfamiliar words. In kindergarten, students learn letter names and letter sounds and are expected to begin using letter sounds during shared reading and writing before they are taught any sight words. In first grade, students learn the most common consonant and vowel patterns and apply these to decoding and spelling words. In second grade, the focus is on less-common vowel patterns and all of the patterns taught in first grade are reviewed. Students also learn that some vowels have two or more common patterns and learn to distinguish these as they read and write words in Reading/Writing Rhymes lessons. In third grade, students continue to work with complex vowel patterns and are taught explicitly how to combine their visual checking with vowel patterns to spell words correctly in an activity called What Looks Right? Common prefixes and suffixes are taught, and students learn to use these morphemic parts to decode, spell, and access meanings for polysyllabic words. This emphasis on using morphemic parts to decode, spell, and build meaning for polysyllabic words is continued in the upper grades as students use roots, prefixes, and suffixes to unlock thousands of polysyllabic words. Explicit instruction of English spelling patterns is evident in all of the *Month-by-Month Phonics* activities. More importantly, perhaps, students are explicitly taught how to use letter patterns to actually decode and spell new words when they are reading and writing.

Month-by-Month Phonics Is Planned and Sequential

It is generally agreed that phonics instruction can be planned and sequential or provided as the need arises. According to the Learning First Alliance (2000):

> "Embedded and incidental phonics are characterized by an implicit approach in which teachers do not use phonics elements in a planned sequence to guide instruction but instead find opportunities to highlight particular phonics elements when they appear in text."

When the chair of the National Reading Panel testified on its findings before a congressional subcommittee, he said:

> "The greatest improvements were seen from systematic phonics instruction. This type of phonics instruction consists of teaching a planned sequence of phonics elements, rather than highlighting elements as they happen to appear in a text." (Langenberg, 2000)

The instruction in *Month-by-Month Phonics* is not embedded, incidental, or implicit, and it does not wait to "highlight elements as they happen to appear in a text." Rather, it is planned and sequential, because during each month at each grade level, there is a planned sequence of lessons with specific letters, sounds, and words provided for the teacher to use. In the program, students begin by learning phonemic awareness, letter names, and letter sounds. They progress to learning digraphs, blends, and vowel patterns in one- and two-syllable words. They continue to progress to decode and spell polysyllabic words.

In addition to being planned and sequential, *Month-by-Month Phonics* is also multilevel. While targeting specific phonics/spelling elements, each lesson also provides opportunities for students to learn a variety of important insights about letters and sounds—including some that are easier than the lesson focus and some that go beyond the lesson focus.

In every Making Words lesson, students are encouraged to stretch out words and put the letters together to form words—an activity that helps students develop the segmenting and blending phonemic-awareness skills. The words made in the middle part of a Making Words lesson contain the targeted phonics/spelling element. The first words in each lesson, however, are easier words and allow students to review or relearn previously taught patterns. The last words in every Making Words lesson—including the secret word that can be made with all of the letters—are more challenging words and are included to provide opportunities for advanced students to extend their knowledge of letters and sounds. When teachers sort words in a Making Words lesson, they sort on a variety of levels. Sorting out words that share a root, prefix, or suffix helps students begin to pay attention to these important morphemic parts, even before that becomes a major focus of instruction. Words can also be sorted by beginning letters to support the development of that knowledge for students who haven't quite mastered it yet. Teachers always sort for rhyming words and transfer those rhyming patterns to decode and spell new words. Sorting words and decoding and spelling new words allows all students to notice a variety of patterns and move forward in their understanding of how the English alphabetic system works. Throughout the program, teachers are reminded of how the activities are designed to be multilevel and how to maximize the effectiveness of the activities for students at all different levels of understanding about words.

The National Reading Panel report did not offer any research-based solutions to the problem of students being at different levels in their word knowledge, but the report did acknowledge the universality of the problem and the dilemma all teachers face:

"As with any instructional program, there is always the question: 'Does one size fit all?' Teachers may be expected to use a particular phonics program with their class, yet it quickly becomes apparent that the program suits some students more than others. In the early grades, students are known to vary greatly in the skills they bring to school. There will be some students who already know the letter-sound correspondences, some students who can decode words, and others who have little or no knowledge. Should teachers proceed through the program and ignore these students?" (p. 2-136)

Overview ···

Month-by-Month Phonics is planned and sequential—and multilevel! Each lesson has a focus but also provides something for both late bloomers and early developers. One size never fits all, and teachers must find ways to accommodate the wide range of learners in their classrooms. *Month-by-Month Phonics* provides teachers with the help needed to accomplish this goal.

Month-by-Month Phonics Is Systematic

It is generally agreed that phonics instruction can be systematic or unsystematic. Adams contrasts "systematic phonics instruction" with "emphasis on connected reading and meaning" (p. 42) and with "meaning emphasis, language instruction, and connected reading" (p. 49). The instruction in *Month-by-Month Phonics* is systematic because a separate time slot is set aside each day for teaching phonics. During this time, the focus is on phonics and word study, rather than on the other essential components of a comprehensive literacy program. The instruction in *Month-by-Month Phonics* is also systematic because it includes regular guidance for the teacher in how to coach students to apply the phonics they are learning during connected reading and writing.

What does the research say about the form that systematic phonics instruction should take? Again, we turn to the National Reading Panel report and to Stahl et al. for guidance. The National Reading Panel (2000) report concluded the following:

"In teaching phonics explicitly and systematically, several different instructional approaches have been used. These include synthetic phonics, analytic phonics, embedded phonics, analogy phonics, onset-rime phonics, and phonics through spelling. . . . Phonics-through-spelling programs teach students to transform sounds into letters to write words. Phonics in context approaches teach students to use sound-letter correspondences along with context clues to identify unfamiliar words they encounter in text. Analogy phonics programs teach students to use parts of written words they already know to identify new words. The distinctions between systematic phonics approaches are not absolute, however, and some phonics programs combine two or more of these types of instruction." (p. 2-89)

The National Reading Panel (2000) report went on to conclude that:

"Specific systematic phonics programs are all more effective than non-phonics programs and they do not appear to differ significantly from each other in their effectiveness." (p. 2-132)

Stahl, Duffy-Hester, and Stahl (1998) discuss two kinds of "early and systematic phonics instruction" (p. 344): traditional and contemporary. Making Words, one of the main kinds of phonics instruction in *Month-by-Month Phonics,* was included by Stahl et al. (1998) in the contemporary kind of systematic phonics instruction. The National Reading Panel (2000) report cautioned its readers not to conclude that newer phonics instructional programs are inferior to the ones examined in the report's meta-analyses:

"Most of these [phonics instructional] programs were developed over 20 years ago, providing researchers with more time to study them than recently developed programs. . . . [T]here was no reason to expect these [older] programs to be more effective than [newer] programs not in the set being compared." (p. 2-105)

Some people associate systematic phonics instruction with decodable text because many synthetic forms of systematic phonics instruction include decodable text. The National Reading Panel (2000) did not conclude that phonics instruction must have decodable text in order to be considered systematic. Rather, the panel concluded that research does not support the need for decodable text when teaching systematic phonics:

> "Very little research has attempted to determine whether the use of decodable books in systematic phonics programs has any influence on the progress that some or all students make in learning to read." (p. 2-137)

Recently, questions have been raised again about the best format in which to deliver phonics instruction. The National Reading Panel (2000) report reviewed research on this question and concluded the following:

> "Systematic phonics instruction is effective when delivered through tutoring, through small groups, and through teaching classes of students . . . All effect sizes were statistically greater than zero, and no one differed significantly from the others." (p. 2-93)

The Type of Systematic Phonics Instruction in *Month-by-Month Phonics*

The National Reading Panel (2000) described several different types of effective phonics instruction, including analogy phonics, onset-rime phonics, phonics through spelling, and phonics in context. *Month-by-Month Phonics* combines all of these types of phonics instruction.

Analogy and Onset-Rime Phonics

Both analogy and onset-rime phonics programs teach students to use parts of written words they already know to identify new words. The parts used are the beginning letters (onsets) and the rhyming pattern (rimes). Cunningham did some of the original research that resulted in the *Month-by-Month Phonics* activities early in her career (Cunningham, 1975–1976; 1979; 1980; 1992; Cunningham and Guthrie, 1982). In this research, analogy-based decoding strategies were investigated and found to be effective in teaching students to decode words. Recently, several research reviews have affirmed analogy strategies, along with other strategies, as effective ways to teach decoding.

In onset-rime phonics, readers decode and spell a word by dividing the word between the onset and rime, pronouncing both chunks, and blending these two pronunciations together. In analogy phonics, students decode and spell new words by thinking of known words with similar patterns. Here is an example of how these two decoding strategies might work:

Imagine a reader who comes upon the word **primp** for the first time. If this reader knows the sounds usually associated with **pr** and **imp**, she will blend the sounds of these two chunks together to pronounce the word. She has decoded the new word, **primp**, by dividing between the onset, **pr** and the rime, **imp**, pronouncing these two chunks, and recombining them to produce the word.

Now, imagine another reader encountering the word **primp** for the first time. This reader also divides between the onset and the rime and thinks of the pronunciation for **pr**, but this reader doesn't have a pronunciation stored for the **imp** rime. This reader then does a quick search through his word store for words he knows that have the **imp** rime. He thinks of **shrimp** and **chimp** and uses these two known words with the same rime to pronounce the **imp** rime. He then blends the onset, **pr**, with the rime, **imp**, and pronounces the word **primp**. Analogies are likenesses or similarities. When teachers ask students to think of analogous situations, teachers are asking them to think of similar situations. When students decode words by analogy, they use similar words to generate pronunciations for new words.

Many of the activities in *Month-by-Month Phonics* focus students' attention on the onsets and rimes in words and how they can use these to decode and spell new words. During these activities, students learn to use both onset-rime phonics and analogy phonics.

During a Making Words lesson, the first part of the lesson, in which students combine letters to spell words, incorporates a spelling approach to phonics. The Sort and Transfer steps of a Making Words lesson incorporate onset-rime and analogy phonics. Words are sorted according to their rimes into rhyming words. Students are then shown new words that have the same rimes as some of the sorted words. They use the sorted words to pronounce new words with the same rimes. To show students how to use rimes to spell words, the teacher pronounces two words that rhyme with some of the sorted words, and students spell the new words using the patterns from the sorted words.

Three other activities used in *Month-by-Month Phonics* also teach students how to use the onset-rime and analogy-decoding strategies. Students use onset and rime patterns to decode and spell new words in Rounding Up the Rhymes, Reading/Writing Rhymes, and Using Words You Know.

Phonics through Spelling

Phonics-through-spelling programs teach students to transform sounds into letters to write words. Making Words, one of the main kinds of phonics instruction in *Month-by-Month Phonics*, was included by Stahl, Duffy-Hester, and Stahl (1998) in the "contemporary kind of systematic phonics instruction that they called a "spelling-based approach." During the first step of a Making Words lesson, students manipulate letters to spell words called out by the teacher. This is clearly a spelling-based approach to decoding.

In addition to providing students with a spelling-based approach to decoding, every Making Words lesson helps students develop phonemic awareness. **Phonemic awareness** is the ability to mentally manipulate sounds in words, to hear when words rhyme and create rhymes, to segment words into sounds, and to blend those sounds back together to form words. During Making Words activities, students are encouraged to stretch out words and explicitly represent each phoneme they hear with a letter, from left-to-right, through the word. Because these activities teach students to hear the phonemes in words, use letters, and add, delete, and replace letters to spell different words, they also teach phonemic awareness in a way that is consistent with another conclusion of the National Reading Panel (2000):

> "Instruction that taught phoneme manipulation with letters helped normally developing readers and at-risk readers acquire PA [phonemic awareness] better than PA instruction without letters." (p. 2-4)

Other activities in *Month-by-Month Phonics* can also be classified as spelling-based approaches. These include Changing a Hen to a Fox, Word Sorting and Hunting, and What Looks Right?

Phonics in Context

Phonics-in-context approaches teach students to use letter-sound correspondences and context clues to identify unfamiliar words they encounter in text. Using knowledge of beginning-letter (onset) sounds and context is the major purpose of the Month-by-Month Phonics activity, Guess the Covered Word. In this activity, students are presented with sentences and paragraphs in which some words have been covered. They guess what each word is without being able to see any of the letters. Next, the teacher uncovers the beginning letters—all of the letters up to the first vowel. Students now guess words that make sense and have all of the correct beginning letters. Students quickly learn that just guessing at a word is not a very productive strategy but that using both the context and all of the beginning letters will often allow them to come up with the correct word.

Research Supporting *Month-by-Month Phonics* Activities

Since the publication of the Stahl et. al and National Reading Panel research reviews, several studies have been published that support the kind of systematic phonics instruction in *Month-by-Month Phonics*. Davis (2000) found that spelling-based decoding instruction was as effective as reading-based decoding instruction for all of her students but was more effective for students with poor phonological awareness. Juel and Minden-Cupp (2000) observed that the most effective teachers of students who entered first grade with few literacy skills combined systematic letter-sound instruction with onset-rime/analogy instruction and taught these units to apply in both reading and writing. McCandliss, Beck, Sandak, and Perfetti (2003) investigated the effectiveness of Beck's instructional strategy, Word Building, with students who had failed to benefit from traditional phonics instruction. Word Building is very similar to Making Words, Changing a Hen to a Fox, and Reading/Writing Rhymes, three of the phonics instructional activities in *Month-by-Month Phonics*. These researchers found that students who received this word-building instruction demonstrated significantly greater improvements on standardized measures of decoding, reading comprehension, and phonological awareness.

Conclusion

All of the activities in *Month-by-Month Phonics* are supported by research, and the program is explicit, planned, and systematic. Unlike some other explicit, planned, and systematic phonics instruction, the instruction in *Month-by-Month Phonics* has variety, is multilevel to meet the needs of a range of learners, and is motivating for students. The instruction in *Month-by-Month Phonics* is consistent with the conclusion of Stahl, Duffy-Hester, and Stahl (1998) in their review of phonics research:

"Good phonics instruction should not teach rules, need not use worksheets, should not dominate instruction, and does not have to be boring." (p. 341)

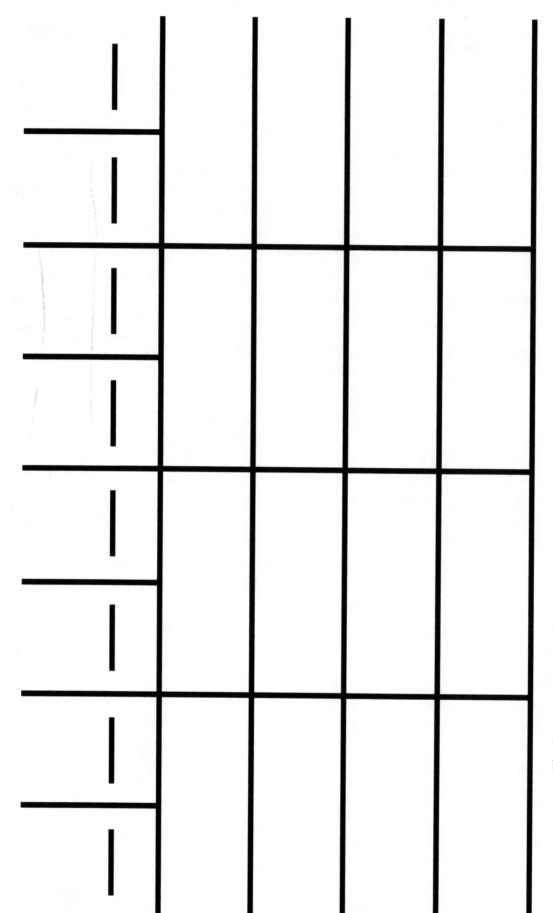

The letters you need to make words tonight are at the top of the page. Write capitals on the back. Then, cut apart the letters and see how many words you can make. Write the words in the blanks.

Making Words Take-Home Sheet

References

Children's Works Cited

A My Name Is Alice by Jane Bayer (Dial, 1984)

All Aboard ABC by Doug Magee and Robert Newman (Dutton Juvenile, 1990)

Angel Pig and the Hidden Christmas by Jan L. Waldron (Dutton Juvenile, 1997)

Animalia by Graeme Base (Harry N. Abrams, 1987)

Annie, Bea, and Chi Chi Dolores: A School Day Alphabet by Donna Maurer (Orchard Books, 1993)

Basketball ABC: The NBA Alphabet by Florence Cassen Mayers (Harry N. Abrams, 1996)

The Best Vacation Ever by Stuart J. Murphy (HarperCollins Publishers, 1997)

Birds Build Nests by Yvonne Winer (Charlesbridge Publishing, 2002)

The Brand New Kid by Katie Couric (Doubleday, 2000)

Bugs and Beasties ABC by Cheryl Nathan (Cool Hand Communications, 1995)

Butterflies Fly by Yvonne Winer (Charlesbridge Publishing, 2001)

Come with Me on Halloween by Linda Hoffman Kimball (Albert Whitman & Co., 2005)

Curious George Learns the Alphabet by Margret Rey and H. A. Rey (Houghton Mifflin, 1963)

Each Peach Pear Plum by Janet Ahlberg and Allan Ahlberg (Scholastic, 1978)

From Apple to Zipper by Nora Cohen (Aladdin Books, 1993)

From Letter to Letter by Teri Sloat (Dutton Juvenile, 1989)

House Mouse, Senate Mouse by Peter W. Barnes and Cheryl Shaw Barnes (VSP Books, 1996)

References $\cdots\cdots\cdots\cdots\cdots\cdots\cdots\cdots\cdots\cdots\cdots\cdots\cdots\cdots\cdots\cdots$

How Do Dinosaurs Eat Their Food? by Jane Yolen (Blue Sky Press, 2005)

How Do Dinosaurs Get Well Soon? by Jane Yolen (Blue Sky Press, 2003)

How Do Dinosaurs Go to School? by Jane Yolen (Blue Sky Press, 2007)

How Do Dinosaurs Say Good Night? by Jane Yolen (Blue Sky Press, 2000)

How I Spent My Summer Vacation by Mark Teague (Knopf Books for Young Readers, 1995)

How Many, How Many, How Many by Rick Walton (Candlewick Press, 1993)

I Love You Because You're You by Liza Baker (Scholastic, 2006)

I Love You, Mom by Iris Hiskey Arno (Troll Communications, 1998)

It's St. Patrick's Day! by Rebecca Gomez (Cartwheel, 2004)

Jennifer Jones Won't Leave Me Alone by Frieda Wishinsky (HarperCollins Publishers, 1997)

A Jewish Holiday ABC by Malka Drucker (Harcourt, 1996)

Jungle Halloween by Maryann Cocca-Leffler (Albert Whitman & Co., 2000)

The Library by Sarah Stewart (Farrar, Straus and Giroux, 1995)

Loud Lips Lucy by Tolya L. Thompson (Savor Publishing House, 2001)

Madeline by Ludwig Bemelmans (The Viking Press, 1939)

Miss Spider's New Car by David Kirk (Scholastic, 1997)

Miss Spider's Tea Party by David Kirk (Scholastic, 1994)

The Monster Book of ABC Sounds by Alan Snow (Dial, 1991)

More Parts by Tedd Arnold (Dial, 2001)

Motherlove by Virginia Kroll (Dawn Publications, 1998)

The Mouse Before Christmas by Michael Garland (Puffin Books, 2001)

My Daddy and I by P. K. Hallinan (Candy Cane Press, 2002)

My Little Sister Ate One Hare by Bill Grossman (Dragonfly Books, 1998)

My Teacher's My Friend by P. K. Hallinan (Ideals Publications, 2000)

NBA Action from A to Z by James Preller (Scholastic, 1997)

The Night Before Easter by Natasha Wing (Grosset & Dunlap, 1999)

The Night Before the Night Before Christmas by Natasha Wing (Grosset & Dunlap, 2002)

The Night Before Summer Vacation by Natasha Wing (Grosset & Dunlap, 2002)

The Night Before the Tooth Fairy by Natasha Wing (Grosset & Dunlap, 2003)

The Night Before Valentine's Day by Natasha Wing (Grosset & Dunlap, 2001)

Parts by Tedd Arnold (Dial, 1997)

Puffins Climb, Penguins Rhyme by Bruce McMillan (Gulliver Books, 1995)

A Rainbow of Friends by P. K. Hallinan (Ideals Publications, 2001)

The Rules by Marty Kelley (Knowledge Unlimited, 2000)

The Runaway Pumpkin by Kevin Lewis (Orchard, 2003)

Saturday Night at the Dinosaur Stomp by Carol Diggory Shields (Candlewick, 2002)

Sea Otters by Avelyn Davidson (Shortland Publications, 1998)

References ·

The Shape of Things by Dayle Ann Dodds (Candlewick Press, 1994)

Shiver Me Letters: A Pirate ABC by June Sobel (Harcourt Children's Books, 2006)

The Snowy Day by Ezra Jack Keats (Viking Juvenile, 1962)

Storytellers by Diana Yurkovic (Shortland Publications, 1998)

The Sweet and Sour Animal Book by Langston Hughes (Oxford University Press, 1994)

The 10 Best Things about My Dad by Christine Loomis (Cartwheel, 2004)

This Is the Dreidel by Abby Levine (Albert Whitman & Co., 2003)

This Is the Pumpkin by Abby Levine (Albert Whitman & Co., 1997)

This Is the Sea That Feeds Us by Robert Baldwin (Dawn Publications, 1998)

This Is the Way We Go to School by Edith Baer (Scholastic, 1990)

Those Can-Do Pigs by David McPhail (Dutton Juvenile, 1996)

Today I Feel Silly and Other Moods that Make My Day by Jamie Lee Curtis (Joanna Cotler, 1998)

Today Is Thanksgiving! by P. K. Hallinan (Ideals Children's Books, 2001)

'Twas the Day After Thanksgiving by Mavis Smith (Little Simon, 2002)

'Twas the Night Before Thanksgiving by Dav Pilkey (Scholastic, 1990)

Wild about Books by Judy Sierra (Knopf Books for Young Readers, 2004)

Woodrow, the White House Mouse by Peter W. Barnes and Cheryl Shaw Barnes (VSP Books, 1995)

Professional References

Adams, M. J. (1990) *Beginning to Read: Thinking and Learning about Print*. Cambridge, MA: MIT Press.

Allington, R. L. (1983) "The Reading Instruction Provided Readers of Differing Reading Ability." *Elementary School Journal*, 83: 549–559.

Allington, R. L. (1991) "Effective Literacy Instruction for At-Risk Students." *Better Schooling for the Children of Poverty: Alternatives to Conventional Wisdom* ed. by M. Knapp and P. Shields, 9–30. Berkeley, CA: McCutchan.

Arens, A. B., Loman, K. L., Cunningham, P. M., and Hall, D. P. (2005). *The Teacher's Guide to Big Blocks™*. Greensboro, NC: Carson-Dellosa.

Bond, G. L. and Dykstra, R. (1967) "The Cooperative Research Program in First-Grade Reading Instruction." *Reading Research Quarterly*, 2: 5–142.

Calkins, L. M. (1994). *The Art of Teaching Writing*. (2nd. ed.). Portsmouth, NH: Heinemann.

Clay, M. (1993) *An Observation Survey of Early Literacy Achievement*. Portsmouth, NH: Heinemann.

Cunningham, P. M. (1975–76) "Investigating a synthesized theory of mediated word identification." *Reading Research Quarterly*, 11: 127–143.

Cunningham, P. M. (1979) "A compare/contrast theory of mediated word identification." *The Reading Teacher*, 32: 774–778.

Cunningham, P. M. (1980) "Applying a compare/contrast process to identifying polysyllabic words." *Journal of Reading Behavior*, 12: 213–223.

Cunningham, P. M. (1992) "What kind of phonics instruction will we have?" *National Reading Conference Yearbook*, 41: 17–31.

Cunningham, P. M. (2000) *Phonics They Use: Words for Reading and Writing*. New York: Longman.

Cunningham, P. M. (2006) "Struggling readers: High-poverty schools that beat the odds." *The Reading Teacher*, 60: 382–385.

Cunningham, P. M. and Allington, R. L. (2006) *Classrooms That Work: They Can All Read and Write*. Boston, MA: Allyn & Bacon.

Cunningham, P. M. and Cunningham, J. W. (1992) "Making Words: Enhancing the invented spelling-decoding connection." *The Reading Teacher*, 46: 106–115.

Cunningham, P. M., Cunningham, J. W., Hall, D. P., and Moore, S. A. (2005). *Writing the Four-Blocks® Way*. Greensboro, NC: Carson-Dellosa.

References

Cunningham, P. M. and Guthrie, F. M. (1982) "Teaching decoding skills to educable mentally handicapped students." *The Reading Teacher,* 35: 554–559.

Cunningham, P. M. and Hall, D. P. (2003) *Reading/Writing Complex Rhymes: Rhymes with More Than One Spelling Pattern.* Greensboro, NC: Carson-Dellosa.

Cunningham, P. M. and Hall, D. P. (2003) *Reading/Writing Simple Rhymes: Rhymes with One Spelling Pattern.* Greensboro, NC: Carson-Dellosa.

Cunningham, P. M. and Hall, D. P. (2008) *Making Words Second Grade.* Boston, MA: Allyn & Bacon.

Cunningham, P. M., Hall, D. P., and Cunningham, J. W. (2000) *Guided Reading the Four-Blocks® Way.* Greensboro, NC: Carson-Dellosa.

Cunningham, P. M., Hall, D. P., and Defee, M. (1991) "Nonability Grouped, Multilevel Instruction: A Year in a First-Grade Classroom." *Reading Teacher,* 44: 566–571.

Cunningham, P. M., Hall, D. P., and Defee, M. (1998) "Nonability Grouped, Multilevel Instruction: Eight Years Later." *Reading Teacher,* 51: 652–664.

Cunningham, P. M., Hall, D. P., and Gambrell, L. B. (2002) *Self-Selected Reading the Four-Blocks® Way.* Greensboro, NC: Carson-Dellosa.

Cunningham, P. M., Hall, D. P., and Sigmon, C. M. (2008) *The Teacher's Guide to the Four-Blocks® Literacy Model: Grade 2.* Greensboro, NC: Carson-Dellosa.

Davis, L. H. (2000) "The effects of rime-based analogy training on word reading and spelling of first-grade students with good and poor phonological awareness" (Doctoral dissertation, Northwestern University, 2000). *Dissertation Abstracts International,* 61: 2253A.

Fielding, L. and Roller, C. (1992) "Making Difficult Books Accessible and Easy Books Acceptable." *The Reading Teacher,* 45: 678–685.

Gentry, J. R. (1987) *Spel . . . is a Four Letter Word.* Portsmouth, NH: Heinemann.

Gentry, J. R. and Gillet, J. W. (1993) *Teaching Kids to Spell.* Portsmouth, NH: Heinemann.

Graves, D. H. (1994) *A Fresh Look at Writing.* Portsmouth, NH: Heinemann.

Hall, D. P. and Williams, E. (2000) *The Teacher's Guide to Building Blocks™.* Greensboro, NC: Carson-Dellosa.

Johns, J. L. (2001) *Basic Reading Inventory.* (8th ed.). Dubuque, IA: Kendall Hunt.

Juel, C.., and Minden-Cupp, C. (2000) "Learning to read words: Linguistic units and instructional strategies." *Reading Research Quarterly,* 35: 458–492.

Langenberg, D. N. (2000, April 13) Findings of the National Reading Panel. Testimony before the U.S. Senate Appropriations Committee's Subcommittee on Labor, Health and Human Services, and Education. *http://www.readingrockets.org/article.php?ID=254.*

Learning First Alliance. (2000, November) Reading glossary. *Every Child Reading: A Professional Development Guide. http://www.readingrockets.org/article.php?ID=174.*

McCandliss, B., Beck, I. L., Sandak, R., and Perfetti, C. (2003) "Focusing attention on decoding for students with poor reading skills: Design and preliminary tests of the Word Building intervention." *Scientific Studies of Reading,* 7: 75–104.

National Reading Panel (2000) *Teaching Children to Read: An Evidence-Based Assessment of the Scientific Research Literature on Reading and Its Implications for Reading Instruction: Reports of the Subgroups* (National Institute of Health Pub. No. 00-4754). Washington, DC: National Institute of Child Health and Human Development.

Routman, R. (1994) *Invitations.* Portsmouth, NH: Heinemann.

Routman, R. (1988) *Transitions.* Portsmouth, NH: Heinemann.

Shepard, L. A. and Smith, M. L. (1990) "Synthesis of Research on Grade Retention." *Educational Leadership,* 47: 84–88.

Stahl, S. A., Duffy-Hester, A. M., and Stahl, K. A. (1998). "Everything you wanted to know about phonics (but were afraid to ask)." *Reading Research Quarterly,* 33: 338–355.

Stauffer, R. G. (1970) *The Language-Experience Approach to the Teaching of Reading.* New York: Harper and Row.

Veatch, J. (1959) *Individualizing Your Reading Program: Self-Selection in Action.* New York: Putnam.

Notes

 CD-104276 • Month-by-Month Phonics for Second Grade

Notes

Notes

 CD-104276 • Month-by-Month Phonics for Second Grade